SCOTT FORESMAN · ADDISON WESLEY

Mathematics

Grade 2

Problem Solving Masters/Workbook

PEARSON

Scott Foresman

Editorial Offices: Glenview, Illinois • Parsippany, New Jersey • New York, New York

Sales Offices: Needham, Massachusetts • Duluth, Georgia • Glenview, Illinois
Coppell, Texas • Ontario, California • Mesa, Arizona

ISBN 0-328-04960-3

8 9 10 V084 09 08 07 06

Joining Groups to Add

Draw the number of missing apples.
Write the missing numbers.

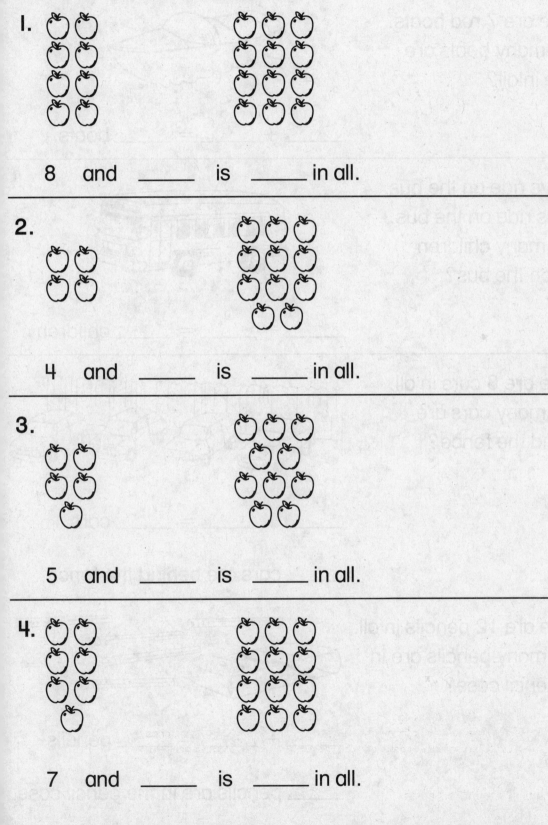

1. 8   and _____ is _____ in all.

2. 4   and _____ is _____ in all.

3. 5   and _____ is _____ in all.

4. 7   and _____ is _____ in all.

Writing Addition Sentences

Write an addition sentence to solve the problem.

1. There are 3 blue boats.
   There are 7 red boats.
   How many boats are
   there in all?

   _____ + _____ = _____ boats

2. 9 boys ride on the bus.
   2 girls ride on the bus.
   How many children
   ride on the bus?

   _____ + _____ = _____ children

3. There are 8 cars in all.
   How many cars are
   behind the fence?

   _____ + _____ = _____ cars

   _____ cars are behind the fence.

4. There are 12 pencils in all.
   How many pencils are in
   the pencil case?

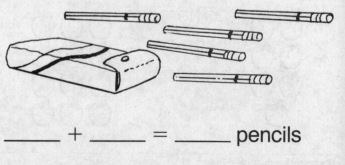

   _____ + _____ = _____ pencils

   _____ pencils are in the pencil case.

Name _____

Write a Number Sentence

5 horses are in a barn.
2 horses are in the field.
How many horses are
there altogether?

_____ horses in the barn   _____ horses in the field

What do you need to find out? _____

                                _____

$\underset{\text{.....}}{5} \oplus \underset{\text{.....}}{2} \ominus \underset{\text{.....}}{7}$ horses _____

---

1. 3 pigs are in the pigpen.
   2 pigs are in the yard.
   How many pigs are there
   in all?   ____ ◯ ____ ◯ _____ pigs

---

2. 5 cows are in the field.
   3 cows are on the road.
   How many cows are
   there altogether?   ____ ◯ ____ ◯ _____ cows

---

3. There are 6 hens in
   the yard. There are
   4 hens in the coop.
   How many hens are
   there in all?   ____ ◯ ____ ◯ _____ hens

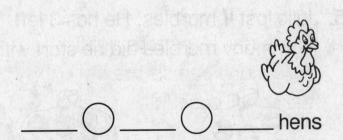

Using the page Have children *read* the story. To help them *understand,* ask children to identify the number of animals and tell what the question is asking.

Taking Away to Subtract

Cross out some stars.
Write the numbers.

1.

6 take away __2__ is __4__.

___

2.

9 take away _____ is _____.

___

3.

10 take away _____ is _____.

___

Circle the group that answers the question.

4. Ishtar sold 2 bracelets. She has 5 bracelets left.
   How many bracelets did she start with?

___

5. Julio lost 4 marbles. He has 3 left.
   How many marbles did he start with?

Comparing to Find How Many More

Compare the number of animals in each group.

Write the numbers.

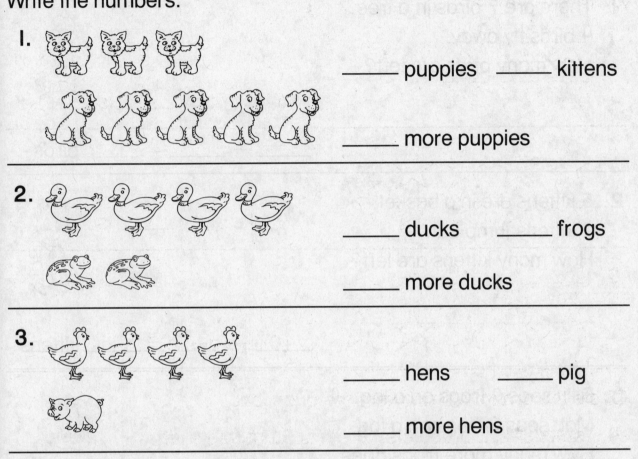

1.

_____ puppies   _____ kittens

_____ more puppies

2.

_____ ducks   _____ frogs

_____ more ducks

3.

_____ hens   _____ pig

_____ more hens

Writing in Math

4. Write a math story with 5 birds and 3 turtles.

_____

_____

_____

Name _____

Writing Subtraction Sentences

Write a subtraction sentence to solve the problem.

1. There are 7 birds in a tree.
   4 birds fly away.
   How many birds are left?

   _____ − _____ = _____ birds

---

2. 5 kittens are in a basket.
   2 kittens jump out.
   How many kittens are left?

   _____ − _____ = _____ kittens

---

3. Billy sees 9 frogs on a log.
   Matt sees 3 frogs on a log.
   How many more frogs does
   Billy see?

   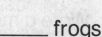

   _____ − _____ = _____ frogs

Circle the answer to the question.

4. Neda has 7 coloring books.   7 coloring books
   She gave some to Felix.
   Which answer tells how many   8 coloring books
   coloring books Neda might have left?   4 coloring books

Name _____

PROBLEM-SOLVING SKILL

Choose an Operation

Circle **add** or **subtract**.
Then write the number sentence to solve the problem.

Kim has 7 pencils.
Bobby has 3 pencils.
How many pencils do
they have in all?

Is this a joining story
or a separating story?

(add)　　subtract　　___7___ $\oplus$ ___3___ $\ominus$ ___10___ pencils

---

1. Pedro has 9 crayons.
   Kate has 4 crayons.
   How many more crayons
   does Pedro have?

   add　　subtract　　_____ ◯ _____ ◯ _____ crayons

---

2. Doug has 6 stamps.
   Shawna has 2 stamps.
   How many stamps do
   they have in all?

   add　　subtract　　_____ ◯ _____ ◯ _____ stamps

Using the page Have students **read** the guiding question. To help them **understand** what they are being asked to do, have them identify the operation that must be used to solve the problem.

Adding in Any Order

Write the addition sentence.
Then write the related addition fact.

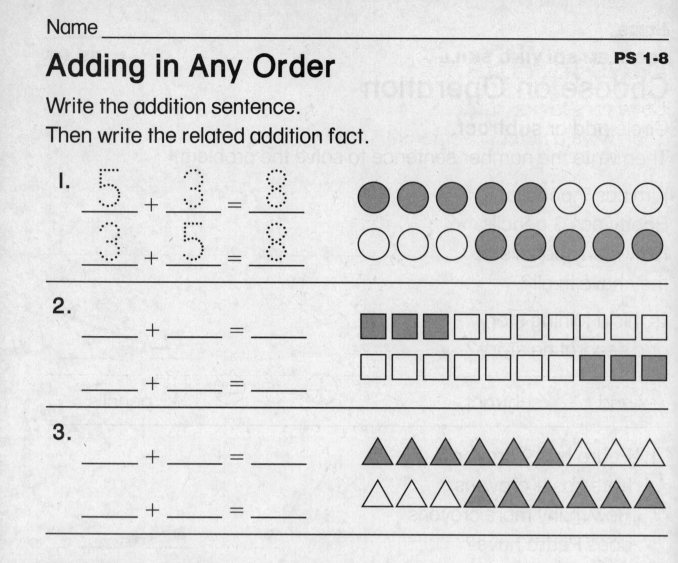

1. $\underline{5} + \underline{3} = \underline{8}$

   $\underline{3} + \underline{5} = \underline{8}$

2. _____ + _____ = _____

   _____ + _____ = _____

3. _____ + _____ = _____

   _____ + _____ = _____

Writing in Math

4. Write the related addition fact.
   Then write a math story for
   one of the number sentences.

   $3 + 4 = $ _____

   _____ + _____ = _____

   _____

   _____

Name _____

Ways to Make 10

Draw dots to make 10.
Then write a number sentence.

1.

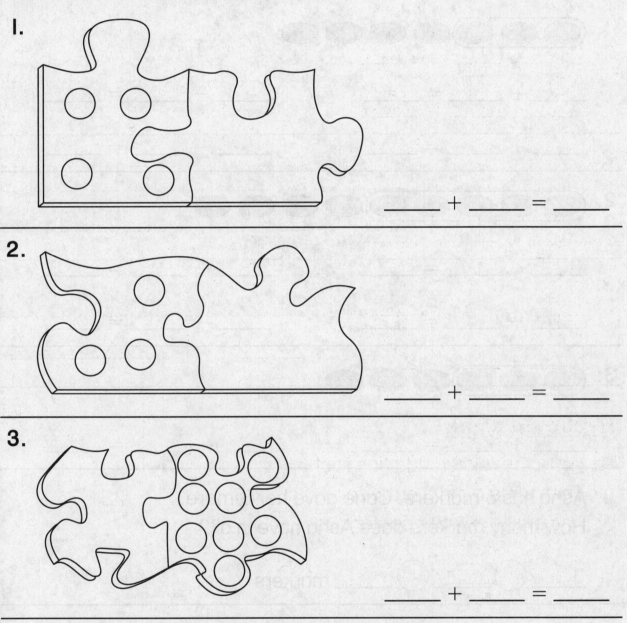

_____ + _____ = _____

2.

_____ + _____ = _____

3.

_____ + _____ = _____

4. Look at the pattern. Find the missing numbers.

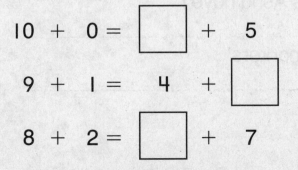

$$10 + 0 = \boxed{} + 5$$

$$9 + 1 = 4 + \boxed{}$$

$$8 + 2 = \boxed{} + 7$$

Fact Families

What facts do these counters show?
Write the fact families.

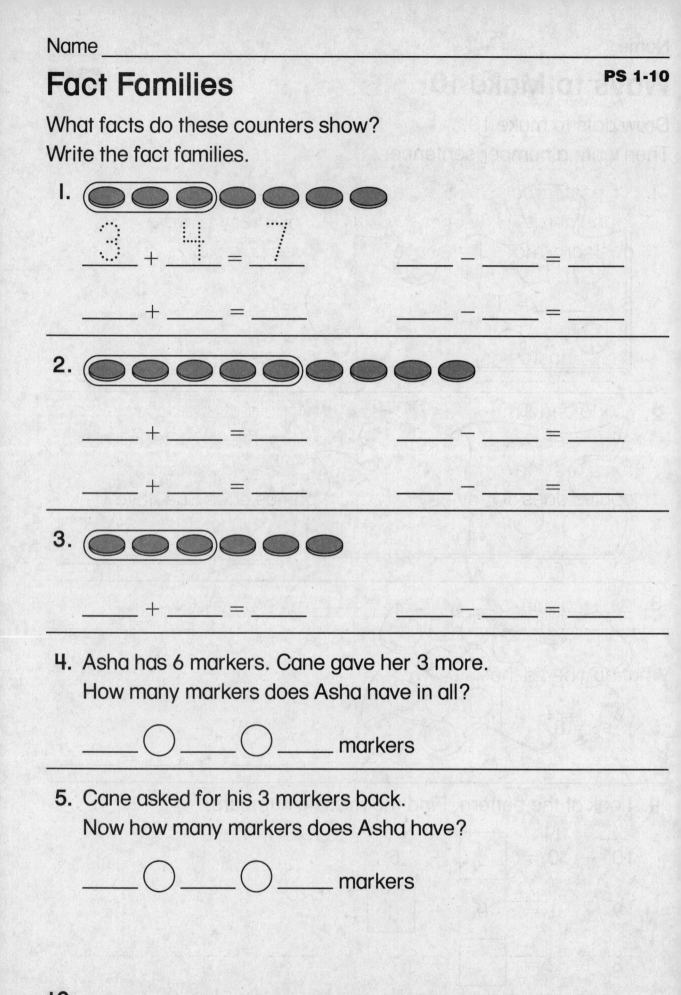

1. __3__ + __4__ = __7__   _____ − _____ = _____

   _____ + _____ = _____   _____ − _____ = _____

2. _____ + _____ = _____   _____ − _____ = _____

   _____ + _____ = _____   _____ − _____ = _____

3. _____ + _____ = _____   _____ − _____ = _____

4. Asha has 6 markers. Cane gave her 3 more.
   How many markers does Asha have in all?

   _____ ◯ _____ ◯ _____ markers

5. Cane asked for his 3 markers back.
   Now how many markers does Asha have?

   _____ ◯ _____ ◯ _____ markers

Name _____

Finding the Missing Part

Solve.

1. Sara and Joey have
   11 postcards in all. Sara has
   8 postcards. How many
   postcards does Joey have?

   8 + _____ = 11

   _____ postcards

2. Zoe and Luis pick 9 flowers
   in all. Zoe picks 6 flowers.
   How many flowers
   does Luis pick?

   6 + _____ = 9

   _____ flowers

3. Marta and Jimmy buy
   10 apples. Marta buys
   5 apples. How many
   apples does Jimmy buy?

   5 + _____ = 10

   _____ apples

4. Mario and Sue have
   12 games in all. Mario has
   4 games. How many
   games does Sue have?

   4 + _____ = 12

   _____ games

What number is the △ ?

5. ○ = 8

   △ = _____

   ☐ = 11

   ○ + △ = ☐

   _____ + _____ = _____

6. ○ = 3

   △ = _____

   ☐ = 7

   ○ + △ = ☐

   _____ + _____ = _____

Name _____

Frogs and Toads

Write a number sentence to solve.

1. There are 6 frogs in a pond.
   4 more frogs jump in the pond.
   How many frogs are there now?

   _6_ ⊕ _4_ ⊜ _10_ frogs

---

2. A bullfrog frog eats 9 bugs.
   A cane frog eats 7 bugs.
   How many more bugs does the bullfrog eat?

   _____ ◯ _____ ◯ _____ more bugs

---

3. There are 5 frogs near a tree.
   3 frogs jump away from the tree.
   How many frogs are left?

   _____ ◯ _____ ◯ _____ frogs

---

4. A toad jumps 10 inches. A frog jumps 8 inches.
   How many more inches does the toad jump?

   _____ ◯ _____ ◯ _____ more inches

---

5. 3 toads are sitting on a log. 6 more toads come to join them.
   How many toads are on the log now?

   _____ ◯ _____ ◯ _____ toads

Using the page To help children *plan* and *solve* each problem, have them underline words that are clues for addition or subtraction.

Name _____

Counting On

Use the number line to solve.
Write the number of jumps.
Count on to find the sum.

$$\longleftarrow \overset{\mid}{0}\ \overset{\mid}{1}\ \overset{\mid}{2}\ \overset{\mid}{3}\ \overset{\mid}{4}\ \overset{\mid}{5}\ \overset{\mid}{6}\ \overset{\mid}{7}\ \overset{\mid}{8}\ \overset{\mid}{9}\ \overset{\mid}{10}\ \overset{\mid}{11}\ \overset{\mid}{12}\ \overset{\mid}{13}\ \overset{\mid}{14}\ \overset{\mid}{15}\ \overset{\mid}{16}\ \overset{\mid}{17}\ \overset{\mid}{18}\ \overset{\mid}{19}\ \overset{\mid}{20}\ \longrightarrow$$

1. Mary starts at 13. She makes
   2 jumps forward. What number
   does she land on?   13 + _____ = _____

---

2. Jack starts at 11. He makes
   3 jumps forward. What number
   does he land on?   11 + _____ = _____

---

3. Paco starts at 9. He makes
   3 jumps forward. What number
   does he land on?   9 + _____ = _____

---

4. Keesha starts at 15. She makes
   1 jump forward. What number
   does she land on?   15 + _____ = _____

Write a number sentence to solve the problem.

5. Chen is 12 years old. How old
   will he be in 3 more years?

   _____ years old   _____ + _____ = _____

Name _____

Doubles Facts to 18

1. Draw a doubles fact
   with 8 objects.
   Write the doubles fact.

   _____ + _____ = _____

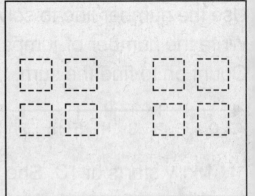

2. Draw a doubles fact
   with 6 objects.
   Write the doubles fact.

   _____ + _____ = _____

3. Draw a doubles fact
   with 14 objects.
   Write the doubles fact.

   _____ + _____ = _____

4. There are 12 oranges in all.
   How many oranges are
   in the bag?

   There are _____ oranges in the bag.

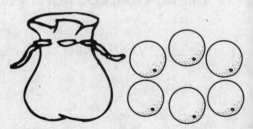

Doubles Plus I

Find the number for each player's shirt.

1. Chenoa's number is between
   4 and 7. Double the number.
   Then add I more to get I3.
   What is Chenoa's number?

_____

2. Jacob's number is between
   7 and I0. Double the number.
   Then add I more to get I9.
   What is Jacob's number?

_____

3. Maria's number is between
   3 and 6. Double the number.
   Then add I more to get II.
   What is Maria's number?

_____

Writing in Math

4. Write a number riddle for the number 7.
   Use a doubles fact in your riddle.

_____

_____

_____

Name _____

Using Strategies to Add Three Numbers

The map shows how many miles from
one place to another.

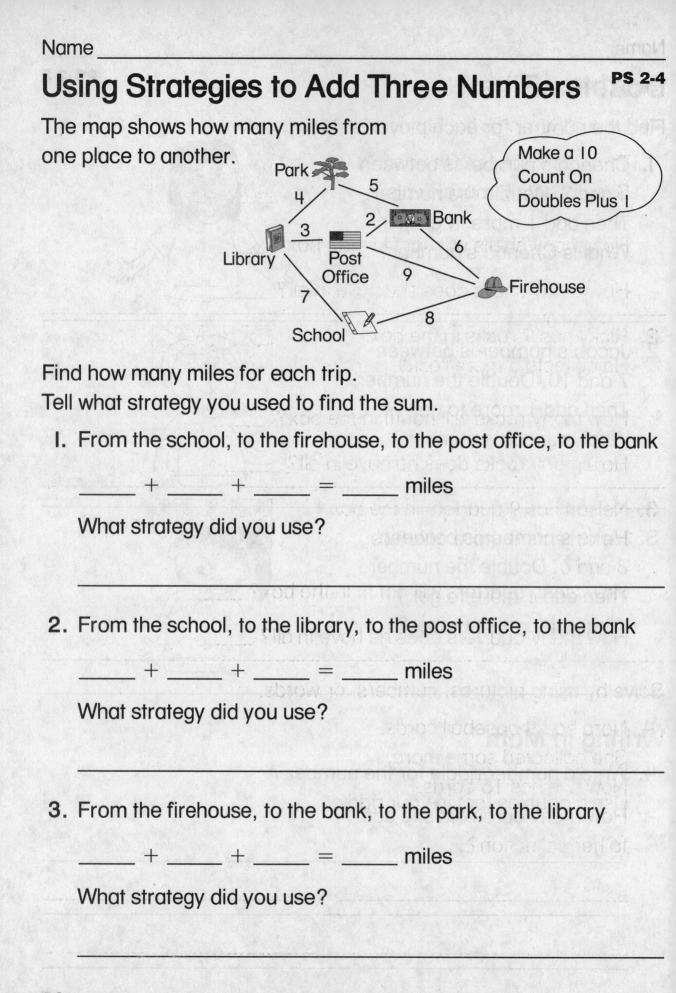

Find how many miles for each trip.
Tell what strategy you used to find the sum.

1. From the school, to the firehouse, to the post office, to the bank

   _____ + _____ + _____ = _____ miles

   What strategy did you use?

   _____

2. From the school, to the library, to the post office, to the bank

   _____ + _____ + _____ = _____ miles

   What strategy did you use?

   _____

3. From the firehouse, to the bank, to the park, to the library

   _____ + _____ + _____ = _____ miles

   What strategy did you use?

   _____

Name _____

Making 10 to Add 9

Help the children fill the sections in their boxes.

1. Tani has 9 shells in the box.
   She collects 7 more shells.

   How many shells will not fit in the box? _____

   How many shells does she have in all? _____

2. Ricky has 9 rocks in the box.
   He collects 5 more rocks.

   How many rocks will not fit in the box? _____

   How many rocks does he have in all? _____

3. Nelson has 9 quarters in the box.
   He collects 8 more quarters.

   How many quarters will not fit in the box? _____

   How many quarters does he have in all? _____

Solve by using pictures, numbers, or words.

4. Nora had 9 baseball cards.
   She collected some more.
   Now she has 15 cards.
   How many cards did she add
   to her collection?

   _____

   _____

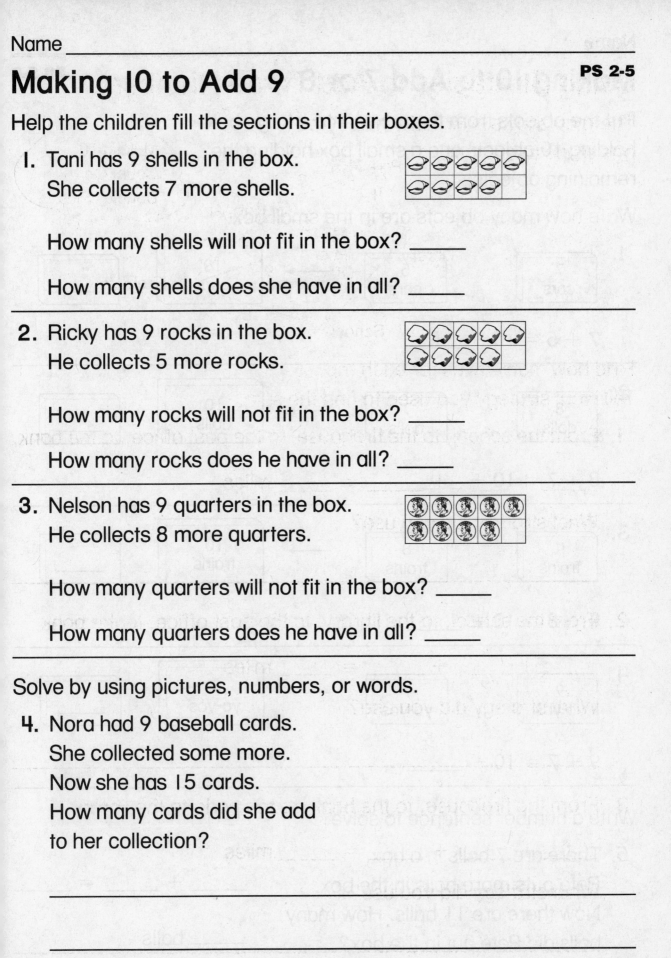

Making 10 to Add 7 or 8

Put the objects from the boxes into a large box holding 10 objects and a small box holding the remaining objects.

Write how many objects are in the small box.

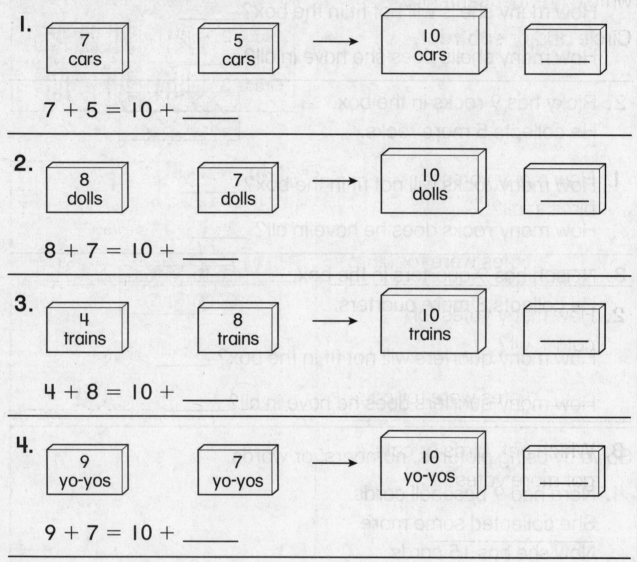

1. | 7 cars | | 5 cars | → | 10 cars | | _____ |

$7 + 5 = 10 + \underline{\hspace{1cm}}$

2. | 8 dolls | | 7 dolls | → | 10 dolls | | _____ |

$8 + 7 = 10 + \underline{\hspace{1cm}}$

3. | 4 trains | | 8 trains | → | 10 trains | | _____ |

$4 + 8 = 10 + \underline{\hspace{1cm}}$

4. | 9 yo-yos | | 7 yo-yos | → | 10 yo-yos | | _____ |

$9 + 7 = 10 + \underline{\hspace{1cm}}$

Write a number sentence to solve.

5. There are 7 balls in a box.
    Pete puts more balls in the box.
    Now there are 11 balls. How many
    balls did Pete put in the box?

    _____ + _____ = _____

    _____ balls

Name _____

PROBLEM-SOLVING STRATEGY
Write a Number Sentence

The children at Smith Street
School voted for their favorite pets.
Use the information in the chart to
write a number sentence.

Circle **add** or **subtract**.

Favorite Pets

	Dogs	Cats	Birds
Grade 1	卌 I	卌 I	III
Grade 2	卌	卌 IIII	卌 II
Grade 3	卌 I	卌	IIII

Plan

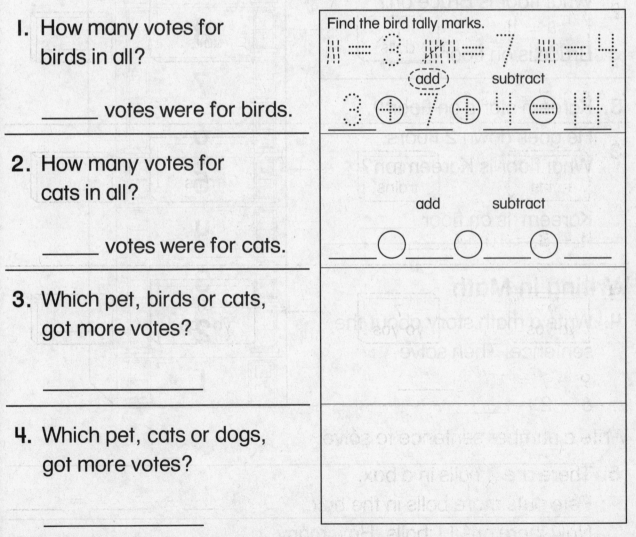

1. How many votes for
   birds in all?

   _____ votes were for birds.

   Find the bird tally marks.

   III = 3   卌 II = 7   IIII = 4
        (add)   subtract

   3 ⊕ 7 ⊕ 4 ⊜ 14

2. How many votes for
   cats in all?

   _____ votes were for cats.

   add   subtract

   _____ ◯ _____ ◯ _____ ◯ _____

3. Which pet, birds or cats,
   got more votes?

   _____

4. Which pet, cats or dogs,
   got more votes?

   _____

Using the page To help children *plan,* discuss which tally marks to use for each exercise. Then have them count
the tallies and write a number sentence to *solve* the problem.

Counting Back

Use the picture of the building to help you solve.

1. Tracy starts on floor 7.
   She goes down 1 floor.
   What floor is Tracy on?

   Tracy is on floor _____.

2. Bruce starts on floor 3.
   He goes down 2 floors.
   What floor is Bruce on?

   Bruce is on floor _____.

3. Kareem starts on floor 9.
   He goes down 2 floors.
   What floor is Kareem on?

   Kareem is on floor _____.

Writing in Math

4. Write a math story about the sentence. Then solve.

   $6 - 2 =$ _____

_____

_____

_____

Thinking Doubles to Subtract

Each basket should have the same amount of fruit.
Draw the fruit. Write how many are in each basket.
Then write a subtraction sentence using doubles.

1. There are 8 apples in all.

_____ apples are in one basket.

_____ apples are in the other basket.

_____ − _____ = _____

_____

2. There are 12 pears in all.

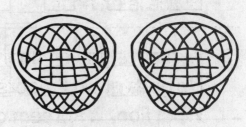

_____ pears are in one basket.

_____ pears are in the other basket.

_____ − _____ = _____

_____

Problem Solving *Writing in Math*

Write a subtraction story about
the cherries in the baskets.

_____

_____

_____

Thinking Addition to Subtract

Color some shapes red. Color some shapes blue. Write the parts and the whole. Write an addition and a subtraction sentence to go with each.

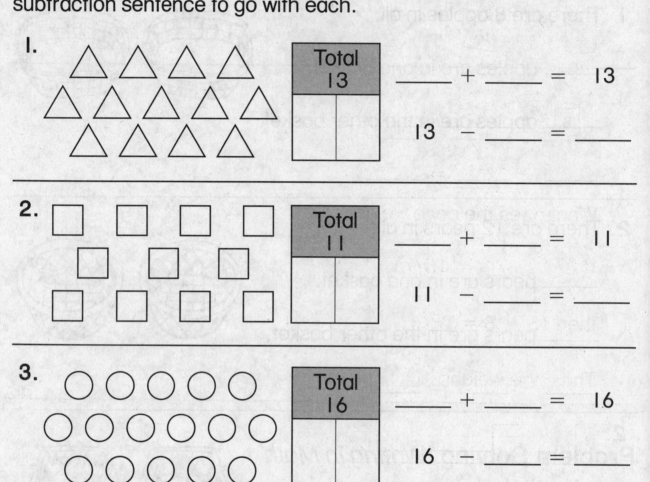

1.

Total 13

_____ + _____ = 13

13 − _____ = _____

2.

Total 11

_____ + _____ = 11

11 − _____ = _____

3.

Total 16

_____ + _____ = 16

16 − _____ = _____

4. Pam picked 2 balls out of the basket. Her score was 14. Color the balls she picked.

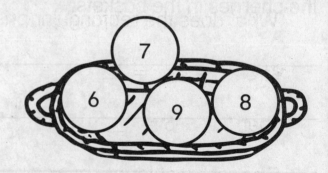

Name _____

Using Data from a Picture

Use the shapes to solve each problem.
Find and write the missing number.

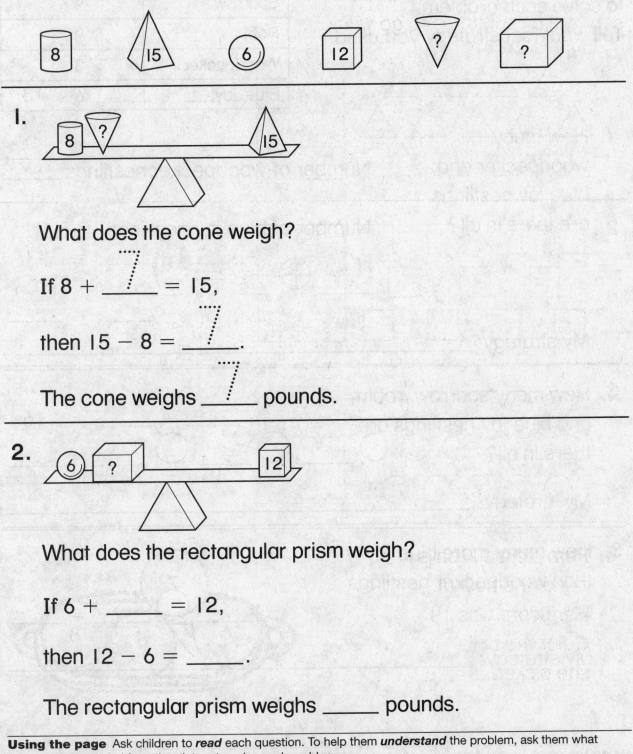

1.

What does the cone weigh?

If 8 + __7__ = 15,

then 15 − 8 = __7__ .

The cone weighs __7__ pounds.

2.

What does the rectangular prism weigh?

If 6 + _____ = 12,

then 12 − 6 = _____ .

The rectangular prism weighs _____ pounds.

Using the page Ask children to *read* each question. To help them *understand* the problem, ask them what information is needed from the picture to solve each problem.

Name _____

Baby Birds

Use the chart.
Write a number sentence
to solve each problem.
Tell what fact strategy you used.

Bird	Number of Nestlings
Sparrow	4
Robin	4
Woodpecker	3
Blue Jay	6

1. How many
   woodpecker and
   blue jay nestlings
   are there in all?

   Number of woodpecker nestlings __3__

   Number of blue jay nestlings __6__

   __3__ ⊕ __6__ = __9__

   My strategy: __Counting on__

2. How many sparrow, robin,
   and blue jay nestlings are
   there in all?

   ___ ◯ ___ ◯ ___ = ___

   My strategy: _____

3. How many more blue jay
   than woodpecker nestlings
   are there?

   ___ ◯ ___ = ___

   My strategy: _____

Using the page Have children *look back* and *check* that they used the right numbers from the table.

Counting with Tens and Ones

Crayons come in boxes of 10.
Solve each problem.
Draw your answer.

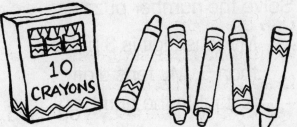

1. Kip has 3 boxes of crayons
   and 4 extra crayons. He gets
   one more box of crayons.
   How many crayons are there now?

   _____ boxes _____ crayons

   _____ crayons in all

2. Tricia has 5 boxes of crayons
   and 8 extra crayons. She gets
   two more boxes of crayons.
   How many crayons are there now?

   _____ boxes _____ crayons

   _____ crayons in all

3. Josh has 6 boxes of crayons
   and 2 extra crayons. He gets
   one box of crayons from his friend.
   How many crayons are there now?

   _____ boxes _____ crayons

   _____ crayons in all

Name _____

Using Tens and Ones

Solve the number puzzles.

1. My tens digit is 3 more
than 5. My tens digit
is double the number
of my ones digit.
What number am I?

_____

2. My ones digit is 2 less
than 8. My ones digit
is 4 more than
my tens digit.
What number am I?

_____

3. My tens digit is 1 more
than the sum of $3 + 3$.
My ones digit is the
difference of $3 - 2$.
What number am I?

_____

4. My tens digit is 1 less
than the sum of $4 + 3$.
My ones digit is 2 more
than my tens digit.
What number am I?

_____

5. My ones digit is 1 less
than 4. My tens digit is the
greatest number of tens
that can be in a number.
What number am I?

_____

6. My tens digit is double
my ones digit. Both of
my digits add up to six.
What number am I?

_____

7. If a softball team has 10 players,
how many teams need to be
formed for at least 68 players?
Draw a picture to solve the problem.

Number Words

Circle all the names and ways to show the number.

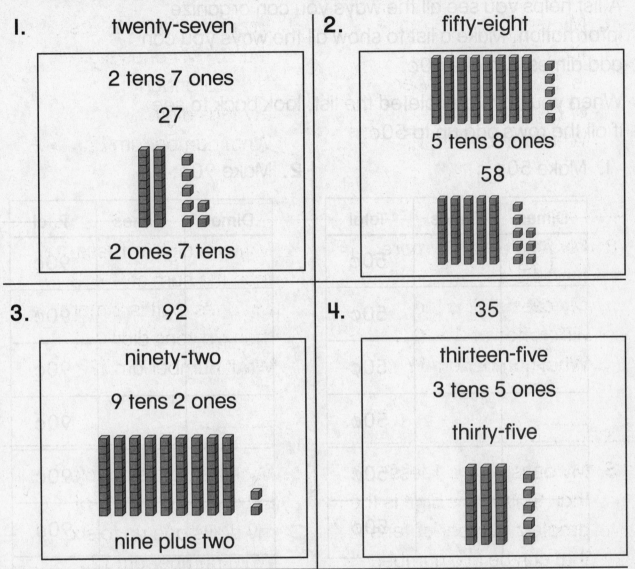

1. twenty-seven

2 tens 7 ones

27

2 ones 7 tens

2. fifty-eight

5 tens 8 ones

58

3. 92

ninety-two

9 tens 2 ones

nine plus two

4. 35

thirteen-five

3 tens 5 ones

thirty-five

What is the number?

5. My tens digit is double my ones digit. My ones digit is the sum of 2 + 2. Write the number word.

_____

6. My ones digit is less than three. My tens digit is greater than seven. If you add the digits, the sum is 11. Write the number word.

_____

PROBLEM-SOLVING STRATEGY

Make an Organized List

A list helps you see all the ways you can organize information. Make a list to show all the ways you can add dimes to make 50¢.

When you have completed the list, look back to see if all the rows add up to 50¢.

1. Make 50¢.

Dimes	Dimes	Total
0	5	50¢
1		50¢
2		50¢
		50¢
		50¢
		50¢

2. Make 90¢.

Dimes	Dimes	Total
		90¢
		90¢
		90¢
		90¢
		90¢
		90¢
		90¢
		90¢
		90¢
		90¢

Using the page To help students *look back* and *check* their answers, ask them whether each row has a total of 50¢ or 90¢.

Name _____

Comparing Numbers

Draw a circle around the correct answer.

1. Ryan picks more than 43 flowers but less than 67 flowers. How many flowers could Ryan have?

   40   60   70

2. Rachel sells less than 30 tickets to a show. She sells more than 15 tickets. How many tickets could Rachel have sold?

   14   26   32

3. The number of baseball cards in Jacy's collection is greater than 70. It is less than 90. How many baseball cards could Jacy have?

   64   78   91

4. Sue picked less than 50 apples. The number of apples she picked was greater than 30. How many apples could Sue have picked?

   27   44   52

What number am I?

5. I am a number less than 59. I am greater than 48. My ones digit is 2 more than my tens digit.

   _____

6. I am a number greater than 48. I am less than 60. My ones digit is 3 less than my tens digit.

   _____

Finding the Closest Ten

Use the information in the chart.
Find the closest ten.

Animals at the Zoo	
Mammals	67
Birds	63
Reptiles	36
Amphibians	51

1. About how many reptiles
    are at the zoo?

    about _____ reptiles

2. About how many birds are at the zoo?   about _____ birds

3. An elephant belongs to the group that is
    closest to 70. What group does an
    elephant belong to?   _____

4. A frog belongs to the group that is closest
    to 50. What group does a frog belong to? _____

5. Color the bar graph to
    show about how many
    animals are at the zoo.

Animals at the Zoo

	Mammals	Birds	Reptiles	Amphibians
70				
60				
50				
40				
30				
20				
10				

6. Some reptiles
    are snakes.
    Which could be
    the exact number
    of snakes?

    26   36   46

    _____ snakes

Before, After, and Between

Match the numbers to the mailboxes.
Use the clues.

Smith   Lopez   Jackson   Ling   Cohen   Russo

1. The number on the Smith mailbox is between 49 and 51. What number belongs on the Smith mailbox?

   _____

2. The number on the Lopez mailbox is one after 23. What number belongs on the Lopez mailbox?

   _____

3. The number on the Jackson mailbox is one before 31. What number belongs on the Jackson mailbox?

   _____

4. The number on the Ling mailbox is between 54 and 56. What number belongs on the Ling mailbox?

   _____

5. The number on the Cohen mailbox is one before 34. What number belongs on the Cohen mailbox?

   _____

6. **Writing in Math** The number on the Russo mailbox is 76. Write a number story to go with 76. Use "one after," "one before," or "between" in your story.

   _____

   _____

Skip Counting on the Hundred Chart

Solve. Use a hundred chart.

1. There are 5 chairs. Each chair has 4 legs.
   How many legs in all? _____ legs

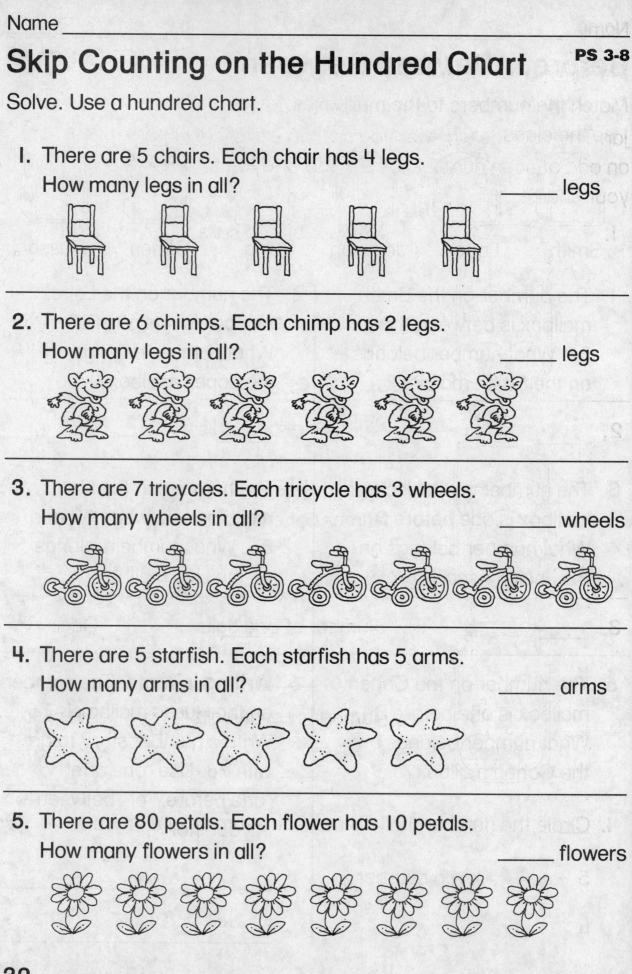

2. There are 6 chimps. Each chimp has 2 legs.
   How many legs in all? _____ legs

3. There are 7 tricycles. Each tricycle has 3 wheels.
   How many wheels in all? _____ wheels

4. There are 5 starfish. Each starfish has 5 arms.
   How many arms in all? _____ arms

5. There are 80 petals. Each flower has 10 petals.
   How many flowers in all? _____ flowers

Even and Odd Numbers

Count the number of odd and even numbers in each jar. Then decide whether you are more likely to pick an odd or even number. Circle **odd** or **even** to show your choice.

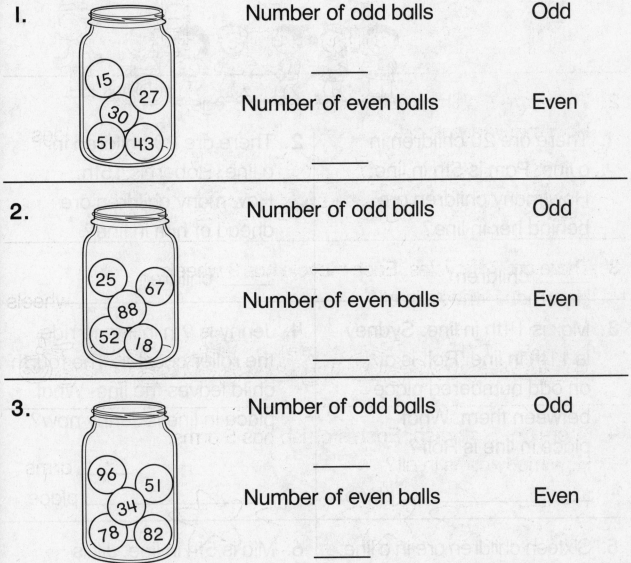

1.
Number of odd balls   Odd

_____

Number of even balls   Even

_____

2.
Number of odd balls   Odd

_____

Number of even balls   Even

_____

3.
Number of odd balls   Odd

_____

Number of even balls   Even

_____

4. Circle the number that will make the sum an even number.

$5 + \boxed{} =$ even number

4   5   6

Name _____

Ordinal Numbers Through Twentieth

1. There are 20 children in a line. Pam is 5th in line. How many children are behind her in line?

   _____ children

2. There are 20 children in a line. Robert is 15th. How many children are ahead of him in line?

   _____ children

3. Max is 14th in line. Sydney is 11th in line. Rolf is at an odd numbered place between them. What place in line is Rolf?

   _____ place

4. Jenny is 9th in line to ride the roller coaster. The fourth child leaves the line. What place in line is Jenny now?

   _____ place

5. Sixteen children are in a line. Pablo is 6th in line. The ninth and tenth place children leave the line. What place in line is Pablo now?

   _____ place

6. Mia is 5th in line. Jill is 8 places after Mia. Frank is 1 place ahead of Jill. What place in line is Frank?

   _____ place

Name _____

PROBLEM-SOLVING SKILL

Use Data from a Chart

This dinosaur measured less than 50 feet.
It measured more than 25 feet.
Its length has more than 3 in the
tens place. Name the dinosaur.

Lengths of Dinosaurs	
Tyrannosaurus	42 feet
Stegosaurus	15 feet
Diplodocus	90 feet
Triceratops	30 feet
Brachiosaurus	75 feet
Allosaurus	38 feet

Think: Which dinosaurs in the chart
were less than 50 feet?

Tyrannosaurus, Stegosaurus,
Triceratops, and Allosaurus

Think: Of these dinosaurs, which
were more than 25 feet?

Tyrannosaurus, Triceratops, and Allosaurus

Which of these dinosaurs has more than 3 in its tens place?

Tyrannosaurus

Use the clues to solve the number riddles.

1. This dinosaur had a length
of more than 50 feet. It
measured less than 80 feet.
Its length has a 5 in the ones
place. Name the dinosaur.

_____

2. This dinosaur measured more
than 30 feet. Its length is an
even number. Its length
has more than 7 tens.
Name the dinosaur.

_____

3. **Writing in Math** Choose a dinosaur from the
chart. Write a number riddle about its length.
Give your riddle to a friend to solve.

Using the page Students should *plan* their approach to each riddle by analyzing the data in the chart, and then
proceed to *solve* each riddle.

Name _____

Dime, Nickel, and Penny

Draw how many pennies, nickels, and dimes each child has.

	Dime	Nickel	Penny
1. Bonnie has 5 coins. This is how she counts the coins: 10¢, 20¢, 30¢, 31¢, 32¢ How many of each coin does Bonnie have?			
2. Leo has 4 coins. This is how he counts the coins: 10¢, 15¢, 20¢, 21¢ How many of each coin does Leo have?			
3. Nick has 6 coins. This is how he counts the coins: 10¢, 20¢, 25¢, 30¢, 35¢, 40¢ How many of each coin does Nick have?			

4. Writing in Math Diana has 5 coins that total 17¢. Draw and label the coins.

Quarter and Half-Dollar

Count the coins.

Do you have enough money to buy the object?

Circle **yes** or **no**.

1.

yes

I have _____ ¢.   no

2.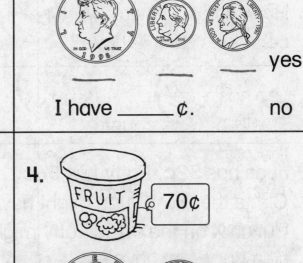

yes

I have _____ ¢.   no

3.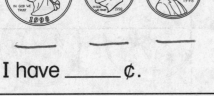

yes

I have _____ ¢.   no

4.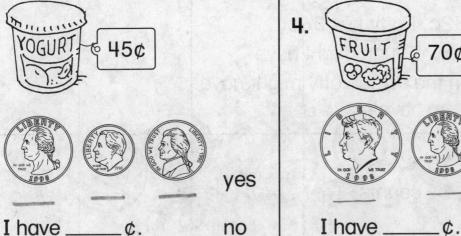

yes

I have _____ ¢.   no

5. You want to buy a bag of trail mix for 99¢.

   Draw the coins you need to buy the bag.

   Use at least one half-dollar and one quarter.

Counting Sets of Coins

1. Mike has 27¢. Anica has 35¢.

   Circle the coins Mike might have.

   Put an X on the coins Anica might have.

2. Juan has 32¢. Patty has 56¢.

   Circle the coins Juan might have.

   Put an X on the coins Patty might have.

3. About how much money do Juan and
   Patty have together? Circle the answer.

   70¢   80¢   90¢

Comparing Sets of Coins

Write how much money each child has.

Compare the coins.

Draw a circle around the child who has more money.

1. Ricardo has
2 quarters, 1 dime,
and 1 nickel.

   _____ ¢

   Millie has 3 dimes
and 3 nickels.

   _____ ¢

   Who has
more money?

   Ricardo

   Millie

2. Eve has 1 half dollar,
2 dimes, and 1 nickel.

   _____ ¢

   Leon has 3 quarters
and 1 nickel.

   _____ ¢

   Who has
more money?

   Eve

   Leon

3. Ramona has
2 quarters and
2 dimes.

   _____ ¢

   Emil has 5 dimes,
2 nickels, and
2 pennies.

   _____ ¢

   Who has
more money?

   Ramona

   Emil

Read the clues. Circle the answer.

4. Alex has more than 40¢.
Alex has less than 60¢.
Which toy can Alex buy?

   55¢

   65¢

   60¢

Name _____

Ways to Show the Same Amount

Draw coins to show two ways that you could pay for the toy.
Use half-dollars, quarters, dimes, nickels, and pennies.

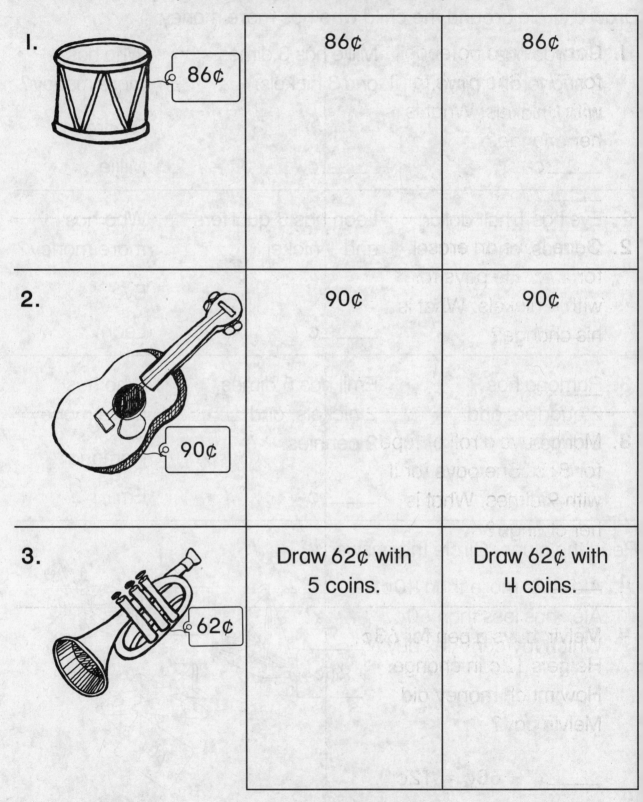

1.	86¢	86¢
2.	90¢	90¢
3.	Draw 62¢ with 5 coins.	Draw 62¢ with 4 coins.

Name _____

Making Change

Solve. Use the workspace to draw or figure out
your answer.

Workspace

1. Carly buys a notebook
   for 74¢. She pays for it
   with 8 dimes. What is
   her change?

   _____¢

2. Gene buys an eraser
   for 27¢. He pays for it
   with 6 nickels. What is
   his change?

   _____¢

3. Maria buys a roll of tape
   for 81¢. She pays for it
   with 9 dimes. What is
   her change?

   _____¢

4. Melvin buys a pen for 63¢.
   He gets 12¢ in change.
   How much money did
   Melvin pay?

   _____¢ − 63¢ = 12¢

Dollar Bill and Dollar Coin

Circle the coin or coins on the right to make the row total $1.00.

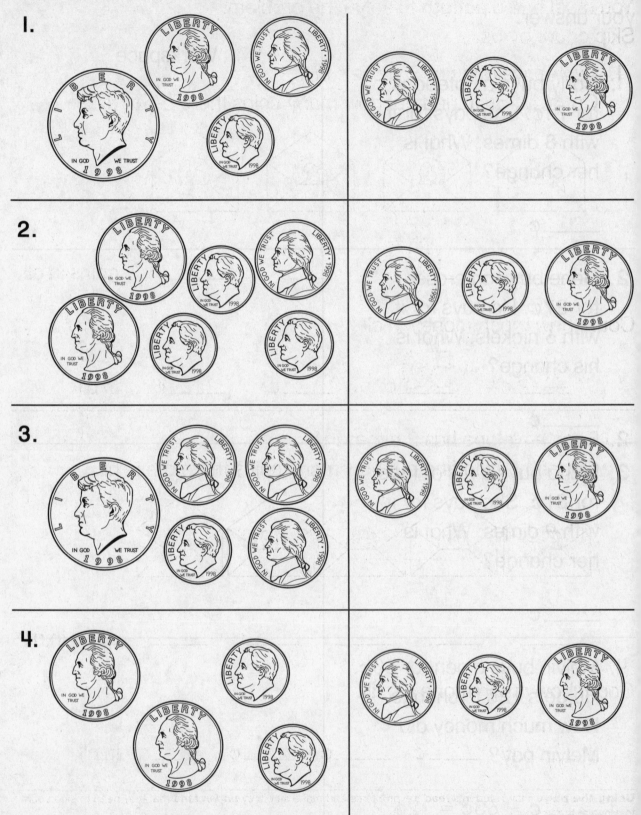

1.

2.

3.

4.

Name _____

Money, Money, Money

You must find a pattern to solve the problem.

Skip count by 5s.

1. Each envelope has 5 nickels in it.

Count by 5s to find out how many coins there are in all.

_5_   _10_   _____   _____   coins in all

Count how much money in all.

_25_¢   _50_¢   _____¢   _____¢   in all

---

2. Each envelope has 2 dimes in it.

Count by 2s to find out how many coins there are in all.

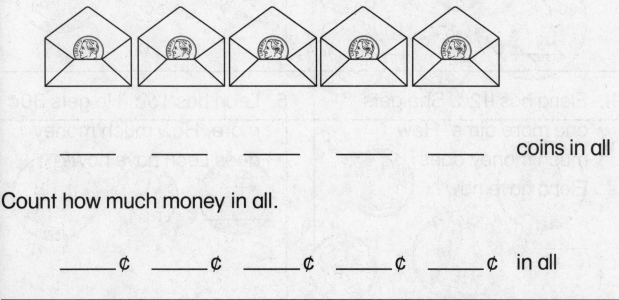

_____   _____   _____   _____   _____   coins in all

Count how much money in all.

_____¢   _____¢   _____¢   _____¢   _____¢   in all

Using the page Have students *read* the problems and make sure they ***understand*** that they need to skip count to arrive at the answers.

Name _____

Adding Tens

Add tens.

1. David has: David finds: How much money does David have now?

_____ ¢   +   _____ ¢   =   _____ ¢

---

2. Karen has: Karen finds: How much money does Karen have now?

_____ ¢   +   _____ ¢   =   _____ ¢

---

3. Brian has: Brian finds: How much money does Brian have now?

_____ ¢   +   _____ ¢   =   _____ ¢

---

4. Elena has 42¢. She gets one more dime. How much money does Elena have now?

_____ ¢

5. Leon has 16¢. He gets 30¢ more. How much money does Leon have now?

_____ ¢

Adding Ones

Circle the coin(s) that answer each question.

1. Keesha has these coins:

Alex has this coin:

Which coin would make their totals equal?

---

2. Ronnie has these coins:

Arnie has this coin:

Which coins would make their totals equal?

---

3. Mandy has these coins:

Gina has these coins:

Which coin would make their totals equal?

---

4. Billy has these coins:

Emily has these coins:

Which coin would make their totals equal?

Adding Tens and Ones

Count the tens and ones.
Write the number in the addition sentence.
Then add.

1. 25 + _____ = _____

2. 34 + _____ = _____

3. 13 + _____ = _____

4. 46 + _____ = _____

Problem Solving *Number Sense*

Circle the digit to make the number sentence true.

5. 21 + 4 ▢ = 67

  6   7   5

6. ▢ 3 + 23 = 76

  3   6   5

Estimating Sums

Each child took two handfuls of beans from the jar below. Estimate the sum of the two handfuls each child took.

1. Jason:

21 and 48 is about _____

2. Sally:

37 and 12 is about _____

3. Abdul:

32 and 57 is about _____

4. Jessica:

28 and 16 is about _____

5. Dawn:

13 and 39 is about _____

6. Mickey:

13 and 17 is about _____

7. Pete:

8 and 13 is about _____

8. Ruben:

28 and 27 is about _____

9. Chen:

43 and 37 is about _____

10. Judy:

14 and 11 is about _____

Problem Solving *Reasoning*

11. Maria has 80¢. She has exactly enough money to buy both toys. How much does the boat cost?

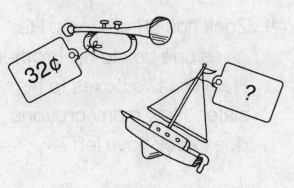

_____ ¢

Subtracting Tens

Each crayon box has 10 crayons. Cross out the crayon boxes given away. Subtract. Write the number.

1. Lea has 38 crayons. She gives one box to her sister. How many crayons does Lea have left?

   38 − _____ = _____

2. Greg has 42 crayons. He gives two boxes to his friend. How many crayons does Greg have left?

   42 − _____ = _____

3. Liz has 26 crayons. She gives one box to her grandmother. How many crayons does Liz have left?

   26 − _____ = _____

4. Zack has 54 crayons. He gives one box to his brother. He gives two boxes to his sister. How many crayons does Zack have left?

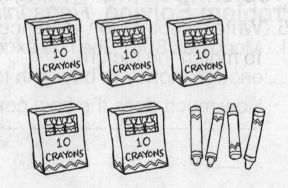

   54 − _____ = _____

Subtracting Tens and Ones

Cross out some tens. Cross out some ones.
Write the number sentence. Subtract.

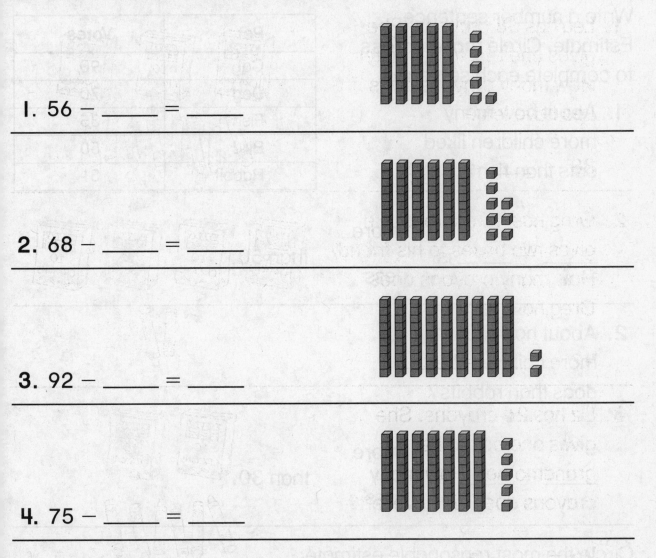

1. 56 – _____ = _____

2. 68 – _____ = _____

3. 92 – _____ = _____

4. 75 – _____ = _____

Problem Solving *Writing in Math*

5. Write a subtraction sentence
   to match the picture.

   _____

Name _____

Estimating Differences

The children at the Elm Street School voted for their favorite pets. Use the chart to answer the questions. Write a number sentence. Estimate. Circle **more** or **less** to complete each sentence.

Pet	Votes
Cat	90
Dog	70
Fish	35
Bird	50
Rabbit	31

1. About how many more children liked cats than fish?

   _____ − _____ is   more   than 50.
                           less

---

2. About how many more children liked dogs than rabbits?

   _____ − _____ is   more   than 30.
                           less

Circle the most reasonable estimate.

3. Another class voted for favorite pets. There were 12 more votes for birds. About how many votes are there for birds now?

   30   50   60

4. 11 children changed their votes from cats to dogs. About how many votes are there for dogs now?

   60   70   80

PROBLEM-SOLVING STRATEGY

Try, Check, and Revise

Use the target to solve each problem.

Vito throws two darts for a score of 40.

On which two numbers did his darts land?

Try two numbers: 24 and 11.

Check: 24 and 11 = 35

35 does not equal 40.

Revise: try 24 and 16.

24 and 16 = 40

So, Vito's darts landed on 24 and 16.

---

1. Susie throws two darts for a score of 50. On which two numbers did her darts land? _____ and _____	**2.** Hannah throws two darts for a score of 20. On which two numbers did her darts land? _____ and _____
3. Tom throws two darts for a score of 60. On which two numbers did his darts land? _____ and _____	**4.** Nick throws two darts for a score of 70. On which two numbers did his darts land? _____ and _____

Using the page Have children *look back* to discover that all sums end in zero. Then have them *check* that the sum of the ones digits equals ten (to make zero in the ones column).

Addition and Subtraction Patterns

Each pattern below has a rule. Find the rule for the
pattern. Then write the next number in the pattern.

1.

| 7 | 11 | 15 | 19 | 23 |

The rule is _____.

The next number is _____.

2.

| 30 | 25 | 20 | 15 | 10 |

The rule is _____.

The next number is _____.

3.

| 8 | 11 | 14 | 17 | 20 |

The rule is _____.

The next number is _____.

4.

| 6 | 12 | 18 | 24 | 30 |

The rule is _____.

The next number is _____.

5.

| 32 | 30 | 28 | 26 | 24 |

The rule is _____.

The next number is _____.

6. Find the pattern. Write the missing numbers.

64, 54, _____ , 34, _____ , _____ , 4

20, 24, 28, _____ , _____ , _____ , 44

Name _____

Finding Parts of 100

Circle the coin or coins that will make 100¢.
Write the number sentence.

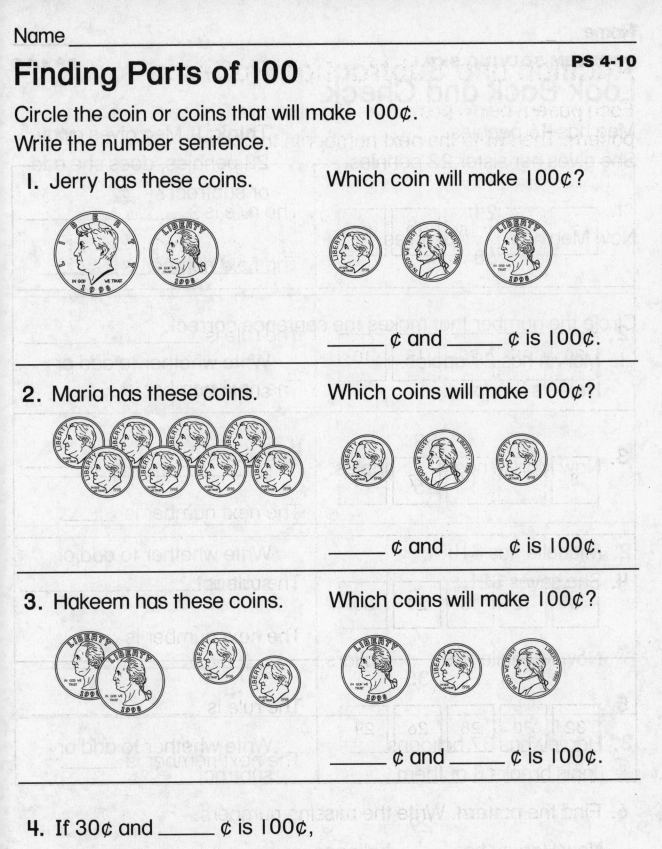

1. Jerry has these coins.

Which coin will make 100¢?

_____ ¢ and _____ ¢ is 100¢.

_____

2. Maria has these coins.

Which coins will make 100¢?

_____ ¢ and _____ ¢ is 100¢.

_____

3. Hakeem has these coins.

Which coins will make 100¢?

_____ ¢ and _____ ¢ is 100¢.

_____

4. If 30¢ and _____ ¢ is 100¢,

then 100¢ take away 30¢ is _____ ¢.

Name _____

Look Back and Check

Meg has 46 pennies.
She gives her sister 22 pennies.

Think: If Meg gives away 22 pennies, does she add or subtract?

Now Meg has (24) / 68 pennies.

subtract _____

Circle the number that makes the sentence correct.

1. Marvin has 29 apples.
He eats 4 apples.

Write whether to add or subtract.

Now Marvin has 33 / 25 apples.

_____

---

2. Michelle has $14.
She saves $21.

Write whether to add or subtract.

Now Michelle has 7 / 35 dollars.

_____

---

3. Harvey has 37 balloons.
Janis breaks 8 of them.

Write whether to add or subtract.

Now Harvey has 29 / 45 balloons.

_____

Using the page Have children *read* each exercise. To help them *understand,* have children answer whether the objects are being added or subtracted.

Take Me Out to the Ball Game!

Baseball Tickets		Gift Stand		Snack Bar	
Adults	$23	T-shirt	$16	Hot Dog	$4
Children	$15	Cap	$8	Soda	$2
Seniors	$21	Bat	$4	Pretzel	$3

Write a number sentence to solve.

1. Dean buys a T-shirt and a cap. How much money does he spend?

____ ◯ ____ ◯ ____

2. A 65-year-old grandfather takes his 7-year-old grandson to the game. How much do the two tickets cost?

____ ◯ ____ ◯ ____

3. How much more would you spend for a T-shirt than a bat?

____ ◯ ____ ◯ ____

4. How much would it cost to buy two hot dogs and a soda?

___ ◯ ___ ◯ ___ ◯ ____

5. How much more does an adult ticket cost than a child's ticket?

____ ◯ ___ ◯ ____

6. Maria buys two T-shirts. How much money does she spend?

____ ◯ ____ ◯ ____

Adding With and Without Regrouping

1. Help the rabbit find the carrots.
   Trace the path that follows the addition
   problems for which you need to regroup.

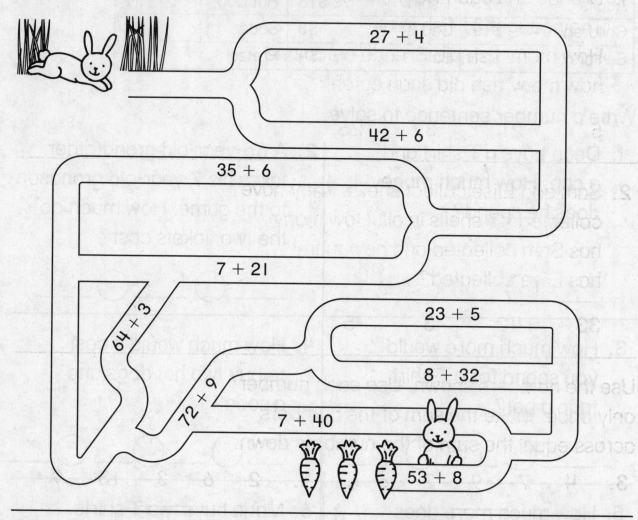

Writing in Math

2. Explain how both pictures show 42.

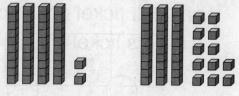

_____

_____

Recording Addition

Read each exercise.
Circle the correct numbers.

1. Brenda and Juan went fishing.
   They caught 31 fish in all.
   How many fish did Brenda catch and
   how many fish did Juan catch?

   5   21   3   26

2. Sam and Elise collect shells. They have
   collected 47 shells in all. How many
   has Sam collected and how many
   has Elise collected?

   33   42   3   5

Use the numbers shown. Use each number
only once. Make the sum of the numbers
across equal the sum of the numbers down.

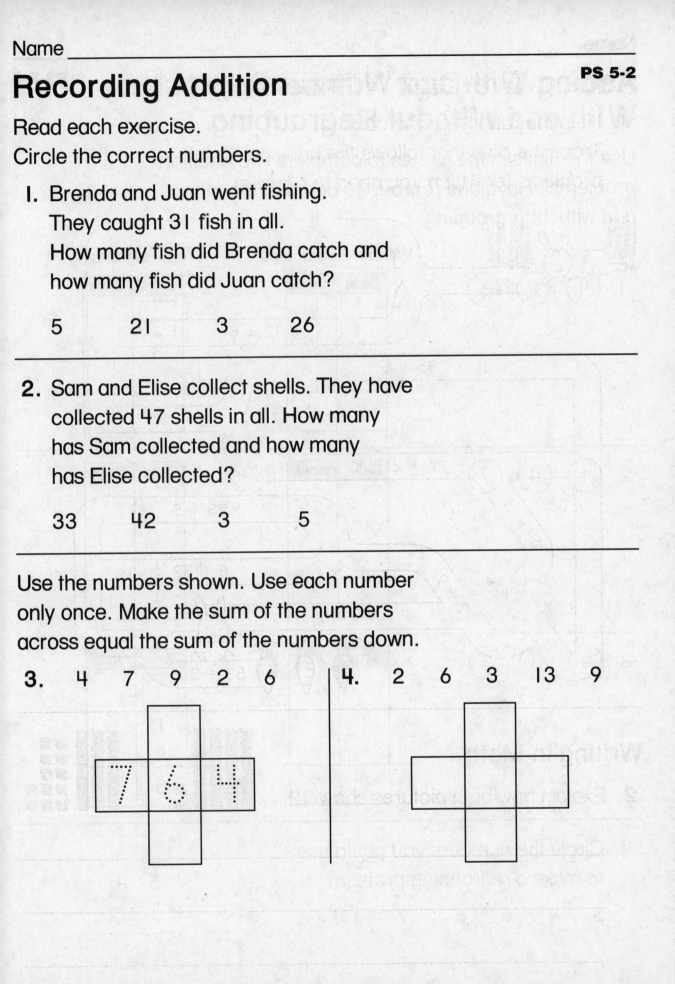

3.   4   7   9   2   6   4.   2   6   3   13   9

Adding Two-Digit Numbers With and Without Regrouping

Use the digits in the circles to complete two addition problems. Have one regroup to add and the other add without regrouping.

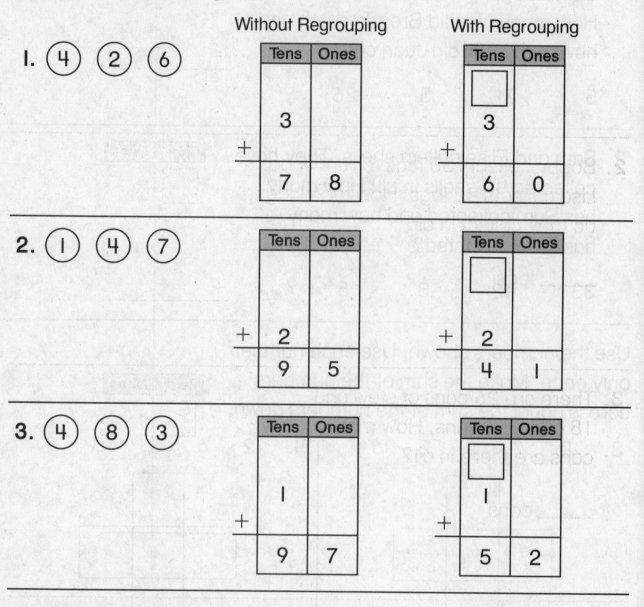

Without Regrouping | **With Regrouping**

1. ④ ② ⑥

Tens	Ones
3	
+	
7	8

Tens	Ones
□	
3	
+	
6	0

2. ① ④ ⑦

Tens	Ones
+	
2	
9	5

Tens	Ones
□	
2	
+	
4	1

3. ④ ⑧ ③

Tens	Ones
1	
+	
9	7

Tens	Ones
□	
1	
+	
5	2

4. Circle the numbers you could use to make a regrouping problem.

   3   4   5   6   7

```
   5  4
+  1  ▢
--------
```

Name _____

Practice with Two-Digit Addition

Write the addition problem. Find the sum.

1. There are 29 girls and 36 boys at camp. How many children in all are at camp?

Tens	Ones
☐	

+

_____ children

2. Bobby collects 35 logs for firewood. Lisa collects 42 logs. How many logs do they collect in all?

Tens	Ones
☐	

+

_____ logs

3. There are 26 cans of stew and 18 cans of beans. How many cans are there in all?

Tens	Ones
☐	

+

_____ cans

4. Write the number for the ■.

$75 + ■ = 95$ ■ = _____

Adding Money

Solve each problem.

Write the highest priced item that the children can buy.

62¢ 48¢ 95¢ 85¢ 76¢ 53¢ 37¢

1. Ian has 17¢.
   Liz has 45¢.
   Together, what can
   they buy?

   _____

2. Sonny has 56¢.
   Tara has 39¢.
   Together, what can
   they buy?

   _____

3. Amy has 31¢.
   Her sister gives her 22¢.
   What can Amy buy?

   _____

4. Your brother has 19¢.
   You give him 29¢.
   What can your brother buy?

   _____

5. Frank has 60¢.
   He gets these coins.
   What can Frank buy now?

   _____

Adding Three Numbers

Look at the sum in the train engine.

Which car is missing from the train? Circle the car.

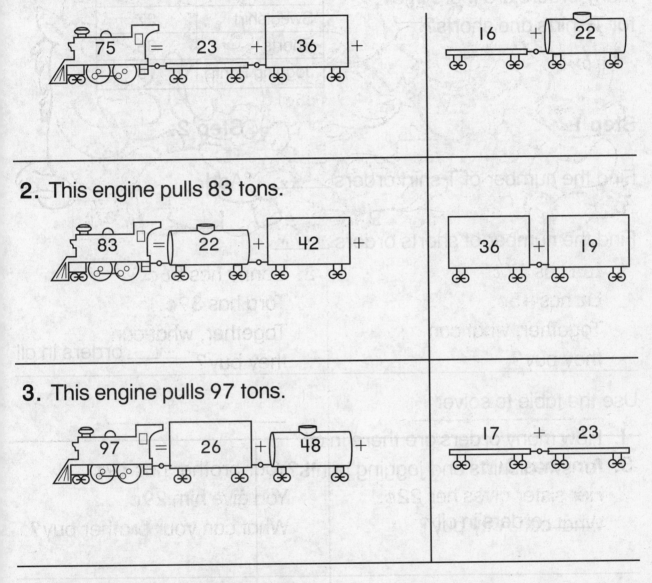

1. This engine pulls 75 tons.

75 = 23 + 36 +

16 + 22

2. This engine pulls 83 tons.

83 = 22 + 42 +

36 + 19

3. This engine pulls 97 tons.

97 = 26 + 48 +

17 + 23

4. Lisa makes a necklace with
   90 beads. She has 40 red beads
   and 30 blue beads. Beads come
   in bags of 10. Circle the bags
   of green beads she will need
   to finish the necklace.

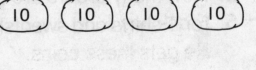

10   10   10   10

Name _____

Use Data from a Table

The second grade classes
ordered gym clothes. How
many orders are there in all
for T-shirts and shorts?

Gym Clothes Orders	
Kind	Number
T-shirt	48
Sweatshirt	27
Shorts	36
Jogging Pants	15

Step 1:

Find the number of T-shirt orders ___48___

Find the number of shorts orders ___36___

Step 2:

Add.

$$48 + 36 = 84$$

___84___ orders in all

Use the table to solve.

1. How many orders are there in all
   for sweatshirts and jogging pants?

   _____ orders in all

2. How many orders are there in all
   for T-shirts and sweatshirts?

   _____ orders in all

Using the page To help children *plan* have them look for the correct item. Then have them write down the
corresponding numbers to *solve* the problem.

Name _____

Estimating Sums

Use the table to solve each problem.

Gifts at the Museum Shop

Posters		Models	
Animals	42	Cars	24
Insects	31	Planes	57
Books		Postcards	
Dinosaurs	28	Cities	17
Flowers	19	Paintings	63

Estimate your answer.

1. About how many posters
   are there in all?   about _____ posters

2. About how many models
   are there in all?   about _____ models

3. About how many books
   are there in all?   about _____ books

4. About how many postcards
   are there in all?   about _____ postcards

5. The museum gets 12 new books
   on flowers. About how many flower
   books are there now?   about _____ books

6. The museum gets 14 new car models.
   About how many car models are
   there now?   about _____ models

Name _____

Ways to Add

Solve. Tell how you solved the problem.

Mental math	Cubes	Paper and pencil	Calculator

1. Mrs. Jones's class goes on a nature hike.
   They see 10 bluebirds and 15 robins.
   How many birds do they see in all?

   _____ birds   I used _____.

2. One group collects 57 leaves.
   Another group collects 38 leaves.
   How many leaves do they collect in all?

   _____ leaves   I used _____.

3. There are 18 boys in Mrs. Jones' class.
   There are 12 girls. How many children are there in all?

   _____ children   I used _____.

4. The class counts 32 squirrels and 15 chipmunks.
   How many animals do they count in all?

   _____ animals   I used _____.

5. Two groups of children collected more than
   70 rocks. How many rocks did each group collect?
   Circle two numbers.

   21   35   40

Name _____

Try, Check, and Revise

You can use try, check, and revise
to solve problems.

Marty has 79 marbles.
Which two bags of marbles did he buy?

Red
18

Blue
25

Green
37

Yellow
42

Try: Choose two bags.   red   blue

Add the numbers.   18 + 25 = 43

Check: Is the sum 79?

Revise: If the sum is not 79,
          try green and yellow.   37 + 42 = 79

So Marty has green and yellow marbles.

---

1. Carol has 62 marbles.
Which two bags of marbles
did she buy?

Try: _____

Check: _____ + _____ = _____

Revise: _____ + _____ = _____

2. Seth has 55 marbles.
Which two bags of marbles
did he buy?

Try: _____

Check: _____ + _____ = _____

Revise: _____ + _____ = _____

Using the page To help students *read and understand* the problem, ask them to explain why Marty can only
buy two kinds of marbles with his money. (Only two numbers will add up to 79.)

Name _____

The Wonderful World of Plants

Mr. Benz planted a garden.

He planted 27 tomato plants and 35 corn plants.

How many plants does he have in all?

$27 \oplus 35 = 62$ plants

Does your answer make sense? Does it answer the question?

Solve.

1. Yola planted 42 bean plants and 27 herb plants.

   How many plants are in Yola's garden?

   _____ ◯ _____ = _____ plants

---

2. On Monday, Yola picked 48 beans. On Tuesday she
   picked 39 beans. How many beans did she pick in all?

   _____ ◯ _____ = _____ beans

---

3. Sue picked 27 red tomatoes from her garden.
   There are still 25 green tomatoes on the plants.
   How many tomatoes is that in all?

   _____ ◯ _____ = _____ tomatoes

Writing in Math

4. Write an addition story about Sue's tomato garden.
   Use two-digit numbers.

Using the page Have children *look back* to make sure they have correctly written each number sentence. Then have them *check* to see if they have answered the question.

66 Use with Lesson 5-11.

Subtraction With and Without Regrouping

Subtract. Color the problems you regroup.

I. 45 – 8 = _____ F	**2.** 62 – 7 = _____ H
3. 91 – 5 = _____ N	**4.** 24 – 6 = _____ M
5. 53 – 7 = _____ S	**6.** 39 – 3 = _____ P
7. 34 – 8 = _____ A	**8.** 81 – 9 = _____ U
9. 57 – 4 = _____ G	**10.** 71 – 2 = _____ T
II. 21 – 4 = _____ I	**12.** 57 – 6 = _____ E

Solve the secret message. Write the letter that goes
with each problem's answer.

____   ____   ____   ____   ____   ____   ____   ____   ____

18   26   69   55   17   46   37   72   86

13. Sandhya baked 25 muffins.
She gave some muffins as a gift.
How many muffins does she
have left?

Sandhya has _____ muffins left.

Name _____

Recording Subtraction

Read each problem.
Circle the correct answer.

1. There are 42 children on the
   playground. 8 children go home.
   How many children are left?   6   50   34

2. Lisa collects 56 leaves in the park.
   She puts 9 leaves in an album.
   How many leaves does she
   have left?   47   65   10

3. Ravi collects 28 acorns.
   He leaves 6 acorns for
   the squirrels. How many acorns
   does Ravi have left?   34   22   6

4. 24 children are playing a game
   of tag. 7 of them quit the game.
   How many children are left
   playing the game?   3   31   17

5. There are 36 children eating lunch.
   7 of them finish eating and go outside.
   How many children are still eating? 29   31   43

6. 12 children are on the monkey bars.
   Some of the children get off the bars.
   Which number tells how many
   children could still be on the bars? 6   12   15

Subtracting Two-Digit Numbers With and Without Regrouping

Help Mr. Potter sort the mail. Subtract.

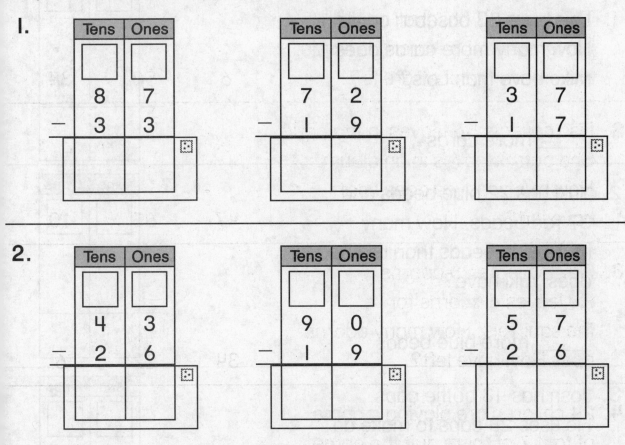

1.

Tens	Ones
8	7
− 3	3

Tens	Ones
7	2
− 1	9

Tens	Ones
3	7
− 1	7

2.

Tens	Ones
4	3
− 2	6

Tens	Ones
9	0
− 1	9

Tens	Ones
5	7
− 2	6

Color the envelopes in which you regrouped red.

Color the envelopes in which you did not regroup blue.

Write the numbers on the envelopes in the correct mailboxes.

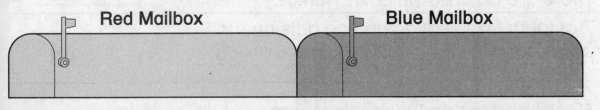

Red Mailbox   Blue Mailbox

Look at the numbers of the envelopes in the Blue Mailbox.

Choose a number that makes each number sentence true.

3. 20 + _____ = 51   4. 45 + _____ = 65

Practice with Two-Digit Subtraction

Write the subtraction problem. Find the difference.

1. Mike buys 65 baseball cards.
Lois buys 23 baseball cards.
How many more cards does
Mike have than Lois?

Tens	Ones
6	5
− 2	3
4	2

_42_ more cards

2. Yuki has 72 blue beads and
37 red beads. How many
more blue beads than red beads
does Yuki have?

Tens	Ones
−	

_____ more blue beads

3. Josh has 43 bottle caps.
He uses 28 caps to make an
art project. How many bottle
caps does Josh have left?

Tens	Ones
−	

_____ bottle caps

Look at the tens and the ones.

4. Which numbers could you subtract without regrouping?

_____

PROBLEM-SOLVING STRATEGY

Write a Number Sentence

There are 35 sleeping bags for the camping trip.
28 children use some of those sleeping bags.
How many sleeping bags are <u>left</u>?

Step 1: Which words help you decide whether to

add or subtract? ___left___

Step 2: Will you add or subtract to
solve the problem?

___subtract___

Step 3: Write a number sentence.

35 ⊖ 28 ⊜ 7 sleeping bags

Tens	Ones
3	5
−2	8
	7

Write a number sentence to solve the problem.

1. 14 boys go on a hike. 18 girls go
on the hike. How many children
go on the hike in all?

14 ◯ ____ ◯ ____ children

Tens	Ones
1	4

---

2. There are 65 crackers in a bag.
The children eat 27 crackers.
How many crackers are left?

____ ◯ ____ ◯ ____ crackers

Tens	Ones

Using the page To help children *plan* and *solve* each problem, have them underline words that help them to
decide whether to add or subtract.

Subtracting Money

Subtract to find the difference.

1. Cara has 46¢.
   She buys the keychain.
   How much money does
   she have left?

   _____

2. Dexter has 90¢.
   He buys the statue.
   How much money does
   he have left?

   _____

3. Corey has 57¢.
   He buys the postcard.
   How much money does
   he have left?

   _____

4. Zena has 75¢.
   She buys the snow globe.
   How much money does
   she have left?

   _____

5. Jacy has these coins.
   Can he buy the pen? Explain.

   _____

   _____

Using Addition to Check Subtraction   **PS 6-7**

Use the numbers in the basket to write a subtraction
problem. Then check your answer using addition.

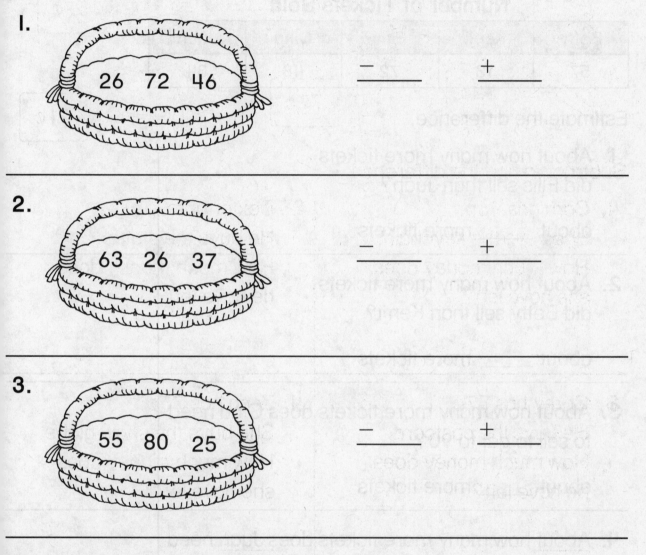

1.   26 72 46

___ − ___   ___ + ___

2.   63 26 37

___ − ___   ___ + ___

3.   55 80 25

___ − ___   ___ + ___

Write the number that makes each
number sentence true.

4. 80 − _____ = 30 + 40   5. 20 + _____ = 40 + 0

   70 − _____ = 50 + 0   10 + _____ = 20 + 70

   60 − _____ = 30 + 10   40 + _____ = 60 + 30

Name _____

Estimating Differences

The children are selling tickets to a school play.
Use the chart to solve each exercise.

Number of Tickets Sold

Betty	Kenji	Ellis	Gina	Juan
57	13	72	48	34

Estimate the difference.

1. About how many more tickets
   did Ellis sell than Juan?

   about _____ more tickets

2. About how many more tickets
   did Betty sell than Kenji?

   about _____ more tickets

3. About how many more tickets does Gina need
   to sell to get to 90?

   about _____ more tickets

4. About how many more tickets does Juan need
   to sell to get to 50?

   about _____ more tickets

5. There are 42 people in the first row at the play.
   There are 28 people in the second row. Estimate
   how many more people are in the first row.

   about _____ more people

Name _____

Ways to Subtract

Solve. Write how you solved the problem.

mental math	cubes	paper and pencil	calculator

1. A coloring book has 45 pages.
   Ted colors 30 of the pages.
   How many pages are left?

   I solved by using _____

   _____.

   _____ pages are left

2. Abbey has 82 crayons.
   Kevin has 38 crayons.
   How many more crayons
   does Abbey have?

   I solved by using _____

   _____.

   _____ more crayons

3. A large box has 38 pencils.
   A small box has 12 pencils.
   How many more pencils are
   in the large box?

   I solved by using _____

   _____.

   _____ more pencils

Writing in Math

4. Gabby solved this problem using cubes.
   Write sentences to explain how she did this.
   Then find the difference.

   $$\begin{array}{r} 28 \\ -13 \\ \hline \end{array}$$

   _____

   _____

Name _____

Extra Information

35 children ride the merry-go-round.

~~There are 23 children that wait in line.~~

18 children ride the Ferris wheel.

How many more children ride the merry-go-round
than the Ferris wheel?

Solve.

$$\begin{array}{r} 35 \\ -18 \\ \hline 17 \end{array}$$

_____17_____ more children

> What information
> is not needed?
> Cross out the
> information you
> do not need.

Cross out the information you do not need.
Then solve the problem.

1. A man sells 47 red balloons.
   Later he sells 26 blue balloons.
   The man also sells 13 puppets.
   How many more red balloons than
   blue balloons does the man sell?

   _____ more red balloons

---

2. The ball toss has 60 stuffed animals as prizes.
   Billy knocks over 12 pins with balls.
   35 of the stuffed animals are given away as prizes.
   How many stuffed animals are left?

   _____ stuffed animals

Using the page To help children *look back* and check each problem, have them identify the information that they
used to solve each problem. Then have them identify the information that they did not use.

Name _____

Here Kitty, Kitty!

A tiger cub named Russell weighs 72 pounds.
His sister, Asha, weighs 56 pounds.
How many more pounds does Russell weigh?

(What is the question asking?)

How much more does Russell
weigh than Asha?

(Subtract to solve.)

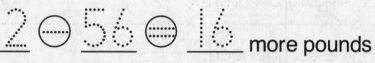 72 ⊖ 56 ⊜ 16 ___ more pounds

---

Solve.

1. A mother tiger eats 68 pounds of meat. Her cub
   eats 13 pounds. How many more pounds of meat
   does the mother tiger eat?

   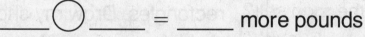 _____ ◯ _____ = _____ more pounds

---

2. There are 47 tigers in one group.
   19 of the tigers are adults.
   The rest are tiger cubs.
   How many of the tigers are cubs?

   _____ ◯ _____ = _____ are cubs

Using the page Have students *read* the problem. Ask them to state the problem in their own words to show that
they *understand* the question.

Flat Surfaces, Vertices, and Edges

Name the solid figure for each description.

Then go on a treasure hunt.

Find and draw one object with the same shape.

I. I have no flat surfaces, vertices, or edges. I am a _____.	**2.** I have 6 flat surfaces. They are all squares. I am a _____.
3. I have two flat surfaces that are circles. You can roll me. I am a _____.	**4.** I have 6 flat surfaces. 4 of these surfaces are rectangles. Draw my shape.

Relating Plane Shapes to Solid Figures   PS 7-2

Write the name of the solid figure.
Then answer the questions.

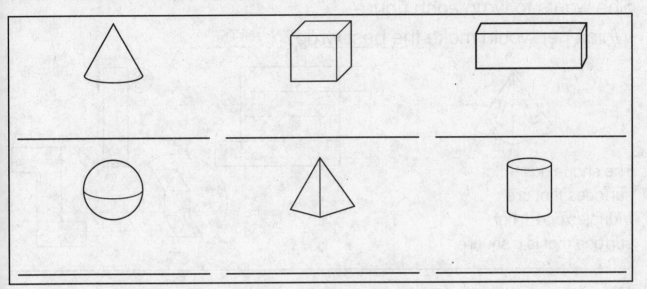

_____   _____   _____

1. Which solid figures have a flat surface that is a square?

_____

_____

2. Which solid figures have a flat surface that is a circle?

_____

_____

3. Name the solid figure that has 4 flat surfaces that are triangles.

_____

_____

4. Marty has one of the solid figures above.
   It has 4 more edges than vertices.
   Which solid figure could he have?

_____

Name _____

Use Data from a Picture

Janet has a glass figure collection.
She wants to wrap each figure.
Which net would make the best wrap?

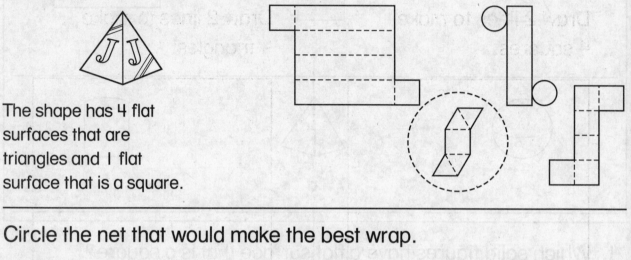

The shape has 4 flat
surfaces that are
triangles and 1 flat
surface that is a square.

Circle the net that would make the best wrap.

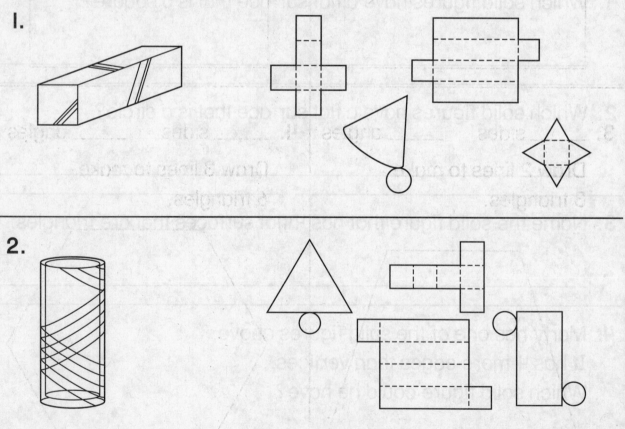

1.

2.

Using the page To help children **check** to see if they chose the correct answer, have them **look back** at the solid
figure. Have children examine the faces of the figure to see if their answer makes sense.

Making New Shapes

Write the number of sides and angles.
Then draw lines to make new shapes.

1. _____ sides _____ angles

   Draw 2 lines to make
   4 squares.

2. _____ sides _____ angles

   Draw 2 lines to make
   4 triangles.

3. _____ sides _____ angles

   Draw 2 lines to make
   3 triangles.

4. _____ sides _____ angles

   Draw 3 lines to make
   6 triangles.

Congruence

Draw a shape that is congruent. Then draw a different shape that is **not** congruent.

1.

2.

Draw a shape that is congruent. Then draw the same shape in a different size that is **not** congruent.

3.

4.

5. Solve.

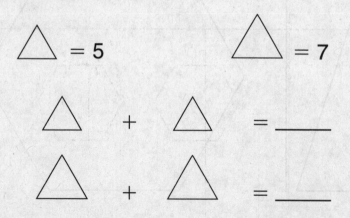

$$\triangle = 5 \qquad \triangle = 7$$

$$\triangle \; + \; \triangle \; = \underline{\quad}$$

$$\triangle \; + \; \triangle \; = \underline{\quad}$$

Slides, Flips, and Turns

Write **slide**, **flip**, or **turn** to tell how the first shape moved. Then circle the position that shows the same move for the next shape.

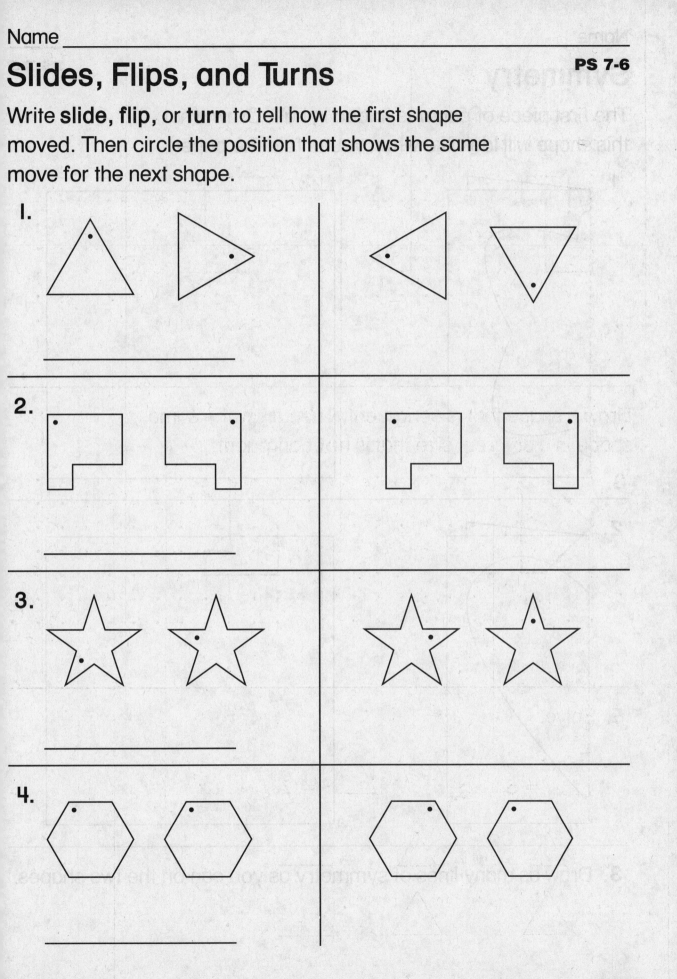

1.

_____

2.

_____

3.

_____

4.

_____

Symmetry

The first piece of paper is folded in half. Draw what this shape will look like when you unfold the paper.

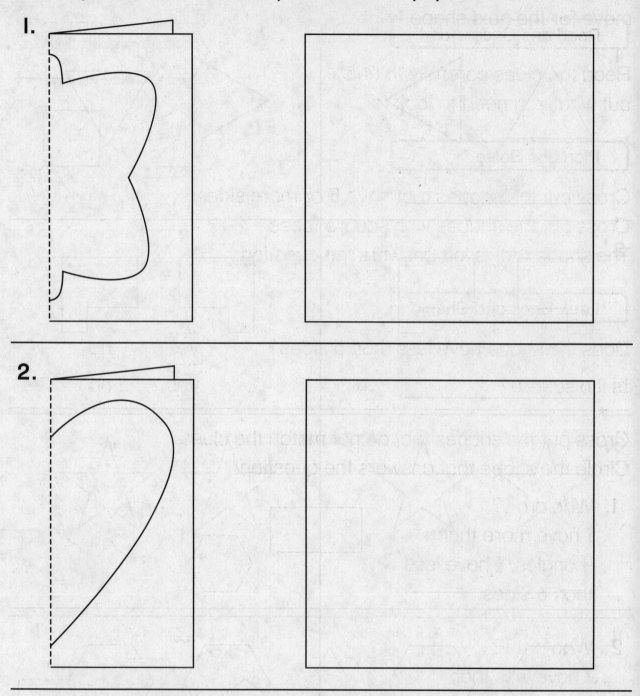

1.

2.

3. Draw as many lines of symmetry as you can on the two shapes.

Use Logical Reasoning

Who am I? I have less than 5 sides. I am not a square.

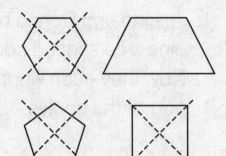

Read and Understand

Read the clues carefully to find
out what you need to look for.

Plan and Solve

Cross out the shapes that have 5 or more sides.
Cross out the shapes with square faces.
The shape that is left answers the question.

Look Back and Check

Does the shape have less than 5 sides?   (yes)   no

Is it a square?   yes   (no)

Cross out the shapes that do not match the clues.
Circle the shape that answers the question.

1. Who am I?
   I have more than
   4 angles. I have less
   than 6 sides.

2. Who am I?
   I have less than
   5 sides. I have
   one line of symmetry.

Using the page To help children **plan,** have them first read each clue and look carefully at the shapes. To **solve,**
have them cross out the shapes that don't match the clues.

Name _____

Equal Parts

Read each story.
Draw 1 or more lines to show equal parts.

1. Justino and Donna baked a pine-tree shaped cookie. Now they each want to eat part of the cookie.

2. Barry, Kika, Oliver, and James share a flower garden. Show each part of the garden.

3. Samantha, Charlie, and Mariko each look out a different part of a window. What might the window look like?

4. An old sign broke in half. Marissa glued the pieces back together. Show Marissa's sign.

5. Biku has three brothers. All 4 children have the same birthday. Show how they shared their birthday cake.

6. 3 friends made a fruit smoothie. Show how much each friend drank.

Unit Fractions

Solve.

1. Marge cuts a pie into 4 equal parts. She eats one part. What fraction of the pie did she eat?

   _____

2. Tony cuts an apple into 6 equal parts. He eats one part. What fraction of the apple did Tony eat?

   _____

3. Becky ate $\frac{1}{6}$ of a pizza.

   Which picture shows the slice of pizza Becky ate?

4. Sasha has $\frac{1}{2}$ of the peanut butter sandwich.

   Marco has $\frac{1}{3}$ of the tuna sandwich.

   Who has more, Marco or Sasha? _____

   peanut butter   tuna

Non-Unit Fractions

Solve.

1. Ken cut a sandwich into four equal parts. Show how he cut the sandwich. Color 2 pieces. How much of the sandwich is colored? Write the fraction.

_____

2. Billy cut the tray of brownies into 8 equal parts. Show how he cut the brownies. Color 6 parts. How much of the tray of brownies is colored? Write the fraction.

_____

3. Maria cut a pizza into six equal parts. Show how she cut the pizza. Color 5 parts. How much of the pizza is colored? Write the fraction.

_____

Estimating Fractions

Name _____

Circle the best estimate.

1. Eddie ate part of a loaf of bread. About how much of the bread is left?

about $\frac{1}{2}$ about $\frac{3}{4}$ about $\frac{2}{3}$

2. Tina poured some juice. About how much juice is left in the pitcher?

about $\frac{3}{4}$ about $\frac{1}{2}$ about $\frac{1}{5}$

3. Cindy made a pie. About how much of the pie is left?

about $\frac{2}{3}$ about $\frac{1}{6}$ about $\frac{3}{10}$

4. Paco made some soup. About how much of the soup is left?

about $\frac{3}{6}$ about $\frac{1}{4}$ about $\frac{2}{3}$

5. Tad made some sauce.

Write the fraction for how much of the jar is filled with sauce. _____

About how much sauce does Tad need to fill the jar?

about $\frac{1}{5}$ about $\frac{1}{3}$ about $\frac{3}{4}$

6. Rosa made a pizza.

Write the fraction for the part that she gave her brother. _____

How much pizza does Rosa have left?

about $\frac{2}{3}$ about $\frac{1}{3}$ about $\frac{3}{4}$

Name _____

Fractions of a Set

Color the objects. Then solve.

1. Olin has 8 buttons. 3 of the
   buttons are red and the rest
   are blue. What fraction of
   the buttons are blue?

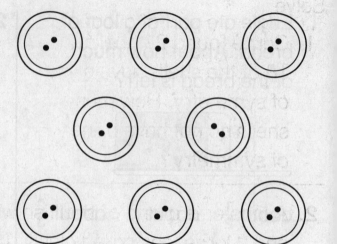

   _____ are blue.

2. Mike has 9 counters. 7 of the
   counters are red. The rest
   are yellow. What fraction
   of the counters are yellow?

   _____ are yellow.

3. Solve. Abbey tosses
   10 pennies on a table.
   4 of the pennies turn up
   heads. The rest turn up tails.
   What fraction of the pennies
   are tails?

   _____ are tails.

PROBLEM-SOLVING APPLICATIONS   **PS 7-14**

Under the Sea

Solve.

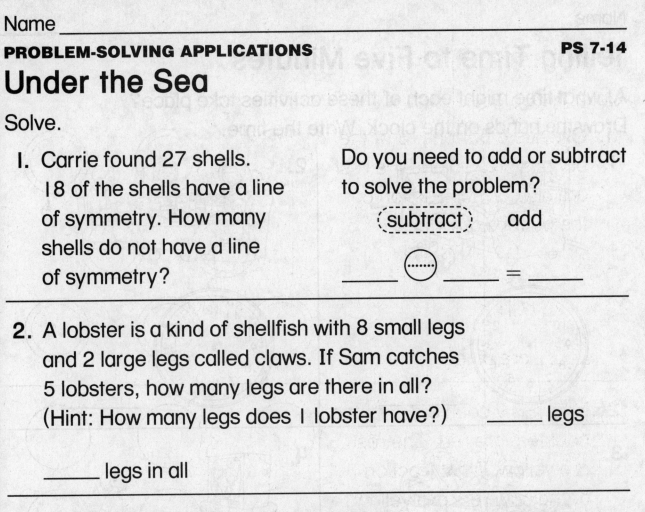

1. Carrie found 27 shells. 18 of the shells have a line of symmetry. How many shells do not have a line of symmetry?

Do you need to add or subtract to solve the problem?

(subtract)   add

_____ ⊙ _____ = _____

2. A lobster is a kind of shellfish with 8 small legs and 2 large legs called claws. If Sam catches 5 lobsters, how many legs are there in all? (Hint: How many legs does 1 lobster have?)   _____ legs

_____ legs in all

3. Jim likes shells that have a cone shape. Circle the shells he might add to his shell collection.

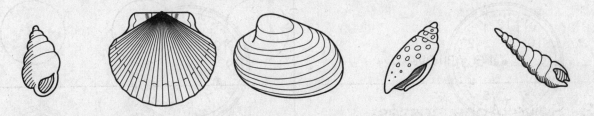

4. Draw a shell that you might like to add to a shell collection. Tell what shape your shell is.

Using the page To help students **understand** the problem, have them **read** each problem first. Then have them plan the strategy they need to use to solve the problem.

Telling Time to Five Minutes

At what time might each of these activities take place?
Draw the hands on the clock. Write the time.

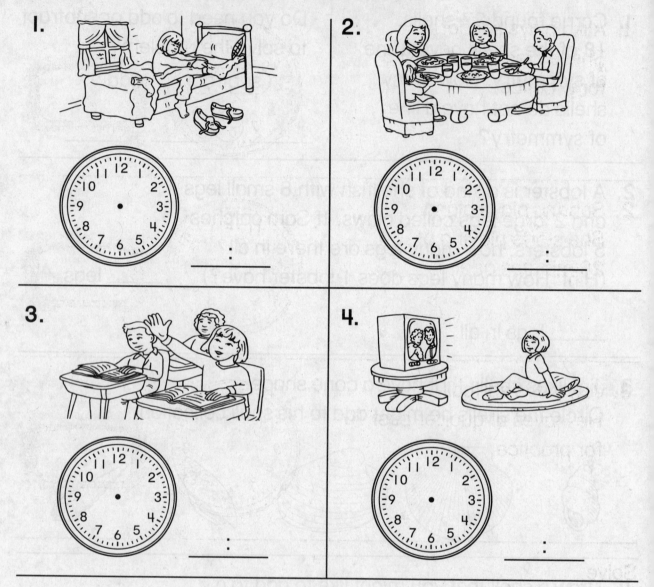

1.

_____ : _____

2.

_____ : _____

3.

_____ : _____

4.

_____ : _____

5. Look at the pattern. Write the time that comes next.

5:00   5:05   5:10   _____ : _____

Telling Time After the Hour

Underline the words in each problem that tell the time.
Then draw the hands on the clock and write the time.

1. Alika plays soccer.
   She leaves at half past 3
   for practice.

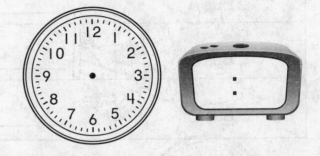

2. Sabrina plays piano.
   She starts playing at
   20 minutes after 1.

3. Jeff plays softball.
   He leaves at quarter past 10
   for practice.

Solve.

4. Martin has band practice at
   half past 5. It takes him
   30 minutes to get to practice.
   At what time does he need to
   leave to get to practice on time?

Telling Time Before the Hour

	Leaves	Arrives Park City
Bus A	_____:_____	_____:_____
Bus B	_____:_____	_____:_____
Bus C	_____:_____	_____:_____

Read the sentences. Write the times in the bus schedule.

1. Bus A leaves at quarter to 7.
   It gets to Park City at 25 minutes before 8.

2. Bus B leaves at 20 minutes before 1.
   It gets to Park City at 5 minutes before 2.

3. Bus C leaves at 10 minutes before 4.
   It gets to Park City at 15 minutes before 6.

4. Nate wants to get to
   Park City by 6:00.
   Which bus should he take? _____

Writing in Math

5. Write 3 ways to say
   the time shown.

_____

_____

_____

Name _____

Estimating Time

Solve.

1. Kim builds a birdhouse.
Sue puts birdseed in the
birdhouse. Who takes about
1 minute to do her activity?

   Kim   Sue

2. Billy plants a garden.
Kenji waters the garden.
Who takes about 2 days
to do his activity?

   Billy   Kenji

3. Sara builds a bookshelf.
Rachel puts books on
the shelf. Who takes about
2 days to do her activity?

   Rachel   Sara

4. Juan brushes his hair while
Matt takes a bath. Who takes
about 1 minute to do
his activity?

   Juan   Matt

5. Ned paints his house.
Berto paints the front door.
Who takes about 5 days to
do his activity?

   Ned   Berto

6. Francine goes to a movie
at the mall. Judy buys a
yogurt at the mall and leaves.
Who takes about 2 hours
to do her activity?

   Judy   Francine

7. Mimi sets the table.
Lara helps make dinner.
Who takes about 5 minutes
to do her activity?

   Mimi   Lara

8. Rodrigo makes lasagna.
Devin eats the lasagna.
Who takes about 1 hour
to do his activity?

   Devin   Rodrigo

Elapsed Time

Draw hands on the clock to show the start time.
Write the end time in the digital clock.

1. Maria walks the dog at 7:00.
   The walk lasts for 30 minutes.
   At what time does she finish?

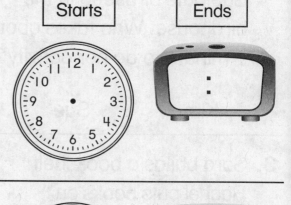

Starts   Ends

2. Ronnie starts to cook dinner
   at 5:00. He cooks for one hour.
   At what time is dinner ready?

3. Betsy gets on the bus at 10:00.
   She rides for 2 hours. At what
   time does the bus trip end?

Solve.

4. Zack starts work at 8:30.
   He leaves for work at 8:00
   and travels for one hour.
   Will he be early or late?

   early   late

5. The concert starts at 2:00.
   Kirk leaves for the concert
   at 1:30 and walks for 15
   minutes. Is he early or late?

   early   late

Name _____

A.M. and P.M.

1. Draw a picture of something you do in the A.M.
   Draw the hands on the clock and write the time.

_____ : _____

---

2. Draw a picture of something you do in the P.M.
   Draw the hands on the clock and write the time.

_____ : _____

---

3. A bus trip starts at 10:00 A.M.
   The ride lasts for 3 hours.
   Does it end in the A.M. or P.M.?

   A.M.   P.M.

Name _____

Using a Calendar

July						
Sunday	Monday	Tuesday	Wednesday	Thursday	Friday	Saturday
			1	2	3	4
5	6	7	8	9	10	11
12	13	14	15	16	17	18
19	20	21	22	23	24	25
26	27	28	29	30	31	

Solve.

1. Olin starts summer camp on July 5. She goes to camp for 14 days. What is the last day of camp?

_____

2. Nell arrives at the beach on July 24. She is at the beach for 7 days. On what day of the week does she leave the beach?

_____

3. Brian goes to soccer camp on July 15. He returns home on Saturday of the next week. What is the date he comes home?

_____

4. Mick goes fishing on July 3. Monique goes fishing on July 5. Both stay for 5 days. Who comes home first?

_____

Name _____

Equivalent Times

Use the schedule to answer the questions.
The shaded boxes show when children have band practice.

Band Practice

	Jason	Alex	Janey	Elisa	Corey
12:00–12:45	▓			▓	
12:45–1:30		▓			
1:30–2:30			▓		▓

1. Which children go to band practice for 45 minutes?

_____

2. Which two children go to band practice for one hour?

_____

3. Ginny has band practice from 12:45 to 1:30. What other child goes to practice during this time?

_____

4. Alice has band practice at the time shown. Who else starts band practice at the same time?

Name _____

Make a Table

Grade 2 has a school supply drawer.

There are 4 crayons, 3 erasers, 6 pencils,

5 paper clips, and 1 ruler.

Read the story again and complete the table.

Use tally marks.

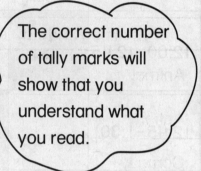

The correct number of tally marks will show that you understand what you read.

School Supplies	
Crayons	IIII

1. How many more pencils than rulers are there? _____ more pencils

2. Which school supply has the most items? _____

3. Which school supply has 5 items? _____

Write the number shown by the tally marks.

4. I _____

5. IHII _____

Using the page Have children *read* the words carefully. Ask them to state the problems in their own words to show that they *understand* what they've read.

Name _____

Recording Data from a Survey

Ricardo asked the children in his school
about their favorite kinds of TV shows.

Use tally marks to help Ricardo
record his data in the chart.

Favorite Kinds of TV Shows	
Animal	
Action	
Comedy	
Cartoons	
Movies	

1. 14 children chose animal shows.

2. There were 11 children who liked action shows.

3. 2 more children chose comedy shows
   than action shows.

4. 1 less child chose cartoons than comedy shows.

5. 15 children said they liked movies the best.
   Then 5 children changed their minds.

6. Suppose 3 more children
   chose comedy.
   What would be the new total? _____ children

Name _____

Using a Venn Diagram

Do you like math, reading, or both?

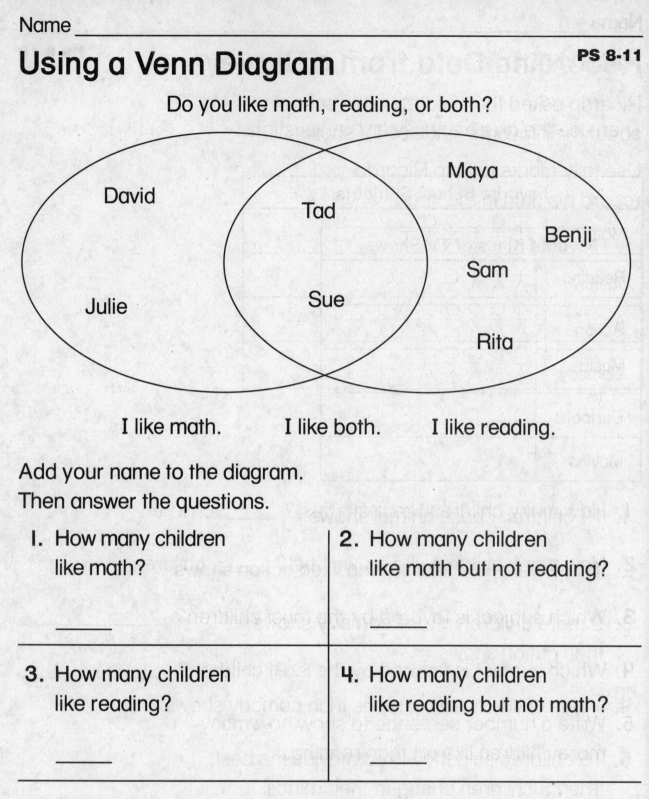

David

Tad

Julie

Sue

Maya

Benji

Sam

Rita

I like math.   I like both.   I like reading.

Add your name to the diagram.
Then answer the questions.

1. How many children like math? _____	2. How many children like math but not reading?
3. How many children like reading? _____	4. How many children like reading but not math? _____

5. Write a question that you could use with
the Venn diagram. Show your results.

_____

_____

Pictographs

Draw a picture symbol next to your favorite subject.
Then use the graph to answer the questions.

Favorite School Subjects	
Math	웃웃웃웃웃웃
Reading	웃웃웃웃
Art	웃웃웃웃웃웃웃웃
Music	웃웃웃웃웃

Each 웃 = I person.

1. How many children like math best? _____ children

2. How many children like music best? _____ children

3. Which subject is favored by the most children? _____

4. Which subject is favored by the least children? _____

5. Write a number sentence to show how many
   more children like art than reading.

   _____ − _____ = _____

6. Write a number sentence to show how many
   more children like math than music.

   _____ − _____ = _____

Name ______________________________

Bar Graphs

PS 8-13

This chart shows the materials children like to use most in art class.

Favorite Art Materials	
Paint	𝍸 ||
Crayons	𝍸 ||||
Clay	|||
Beads	𝍸

I. Use the tally chart to make a bar graph.
Color one box for each time an art material is chosen.

Favorite Art Materials									

0 1 2 3 4 5 6 7 8 9

Writing in Math

2. Do you think the chart or the graph is better for showing the information? Why?

____

____

Name _____

Line Plots

The line plot shows how many times children were able to catch a ball in one minute.

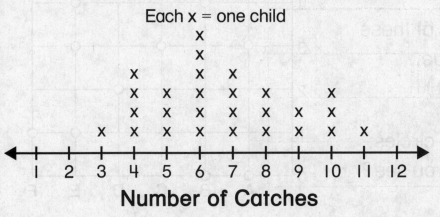

Number of Catches in One Minute

Each x = one child

Number of Catches

Use the line plot to answer the questions.

1. Did more children catch the ball 7 times or 8 times in one minute? _____ times	2. What is the least number of times 4 children caught the ball? _____ times
3. How many times did the greatest number of children catch the ball in one minute? _____ times	4. How many children caught the ball 10 or more times in one minute? _____ children

Circle the answer that is more reasonable.

5. What is the most times someone can bounce a ball in 2 minutes?

5   25

Name _____

Coordinate Graphs

1. Color the circles at these
   ordered pairs red.
   (A, 5) (C, 3) (A, 3) (C, 5)

2. Color the circles at these
   ordered pairs blue.
   (B, 0) (E, 4) (F, 1)

3. Connect the red circles.
   What shape do you see?

   _____

4. Connect the blue circles.
   What shape do you see?

   _____

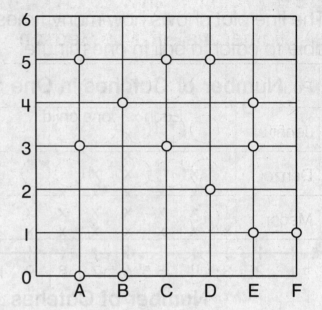

Writing in Math

5. Write a question using some of the leftover circles.

   _____

   _____

   _____

Name _____

Use Data from a Graph

Homeruns Hit This Season

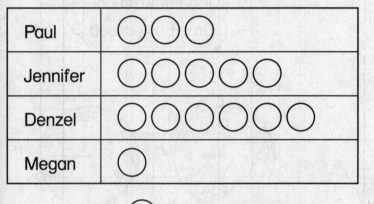

Paul	◯◯◯
Jennifer	◯◯◯◯◯
Denzel	◯◯◯◯◯◯
Megan	◯

Each ◯ = 5 homeruns.

How many homeruns did Paul hit? Count by 5s to count the number of balls.

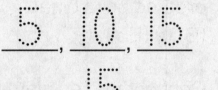

5, 10, 15

Paul hit 15 homeruns.

Use the graph to answer the questions.
Count by 5s to help you.

1. Megan hit 20 homeruns. Draw the rest of the balls in the graph to show how many homeruns she hit.

2. Who hit the most homeruns? _____

3. How many more homeruns did Jennifer hit than Megan? _____ more homeruns

4. How many homeruns did Paul and Denzel hit in all? _____

5. Who hit more homeruns than Megan?

_____

Using the page To help children *plan and solve* each problem, have them count by 5s then write the total number at the end of each row in the graph.

PROBLEM-SOLVING APPLICATIONS

Fly, Butterfly, Fly!

1. A butterfly starts to fly at 3:00.
   It flies for 15 minutes.

   > Find how much time has passed.

   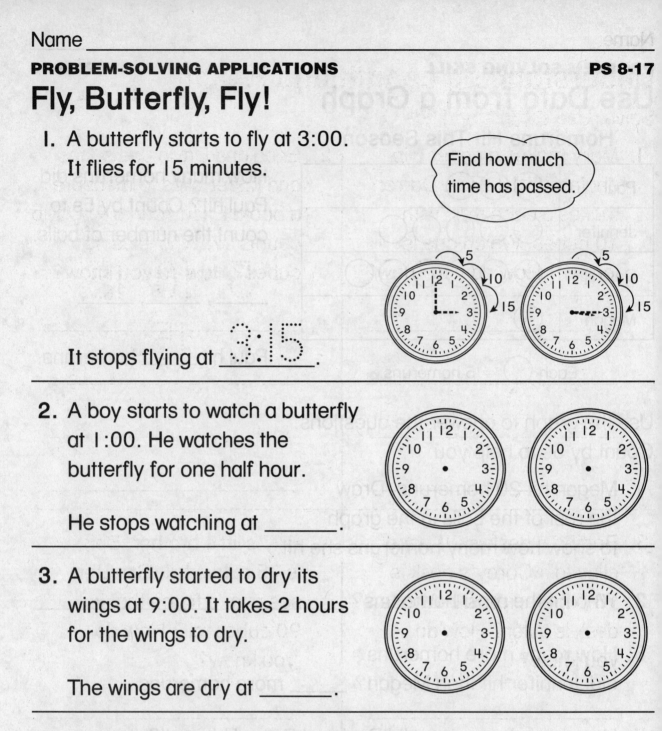

   It stops flying at __3:15__.

2. A boy starts to watch a butterfly
   at 1:00. He watches the
   butterfly for one half hour.

   He stops watching at _____.

3. A butterfly started to dry its
   wings at 9:00. It takes 2 hours
   for the wings to dry.

   The wings are dry at _____.

4. A butterfly rests on a flower for one quarter of an hour.
   Write the time in another way.

   _____

Using the page Have students *look back* at their answers, using an analog clockface to help them *check* the times.

Understanding Length and Height

Solve. Use ⬭ and ▢.

1. Mary makes a paper clip chain with 10 clips. Darren makes a cube train with 10 cubes. Which one is longer? How do you know?

_____

_____

_____

2. Erica and David use cubes and paper clips to measure a book. Erica counts 9. David counts 17. Who is using cubes? How do you know?

_____

_____

_____

3. Bettina's desk is 24 paper clips tall. Corey's desk is 18 paper clips tall. Whose desk is taller? How do you know?

_____

_____

4. Billy's little brother, Ben, is 75 cubes tall. Can Ben see over a fence that is 90 cubes tall? How do you know?

_____

_____

Circle the line that is longer.

5. _____

_____

6. _____

_____

Name _____

Inches and Feet

Use the clues to complete the table.

Then answer the questions.

Pets We Have		Length in Inches
	Rabbit	12
	Ferret	
	Dog	
	Snake	
	Turtle	

1. The ferret is the same length as the rabbit.

2. The dog is 24 inches longer than the rabbit.

3. The snake is one foot shorter than the dog.

4. The turtle is 8 inches longer than the ferret.

5. Which animal is the longest? _____

6. How much longer is the snake than the turtle? _____

_____

7. Laura has a cat that is 13 inches long.

   Jimmy has a cat that is one foot long.

   Who has the longer cat? How do you know?

_____

Inches, Feet, and Yards

Circle the best estimate.

1. About how long is
   a football field?

   about 100 inches

   about 100 feet

   about 100 yards

2. About how wide is
   a window?

   about 3 inches

   about 3 feet

   about 3 yards

3. About how high is
   a flagpole?

   about 8 inches

   about 8 feet

   about 8 yards

4. About how long is
   a pair of scissors?

   about 6 inches

   about 6 feet

   about 6 yards

5. About how high is a fence?

   about 4 inches

   about 4 feet

   about 4 yards

6. A table is 1 yard long.
   A tablecloth is 40 inches long.
   Will the tablecloth fit over the
   table? How do you know?

   _____

   _____

   _____

   _____

Centimeters and Meters

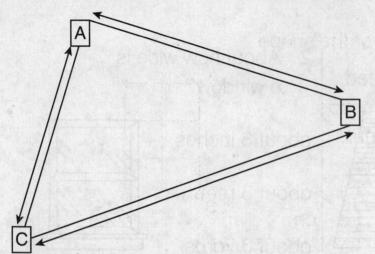

Use a ruler to measure each distance.

1. From A to B is _____ centimeters long.

2. From B to C is _____ centimeters long.

3. From A to C is _____ centimeters long.

4. The total distance from A to B to C

   and back to A is _____ centimeters long.

5. If 1 centimeter stands for 1 meter, what is
   the total distance in meters from A to B to C? _____ meters

Writing in Math

6. A bookcase is 1 meter wide. Will it fit in a space
   that is 75 cm wide? How do you know?

   _____

   _____

PROBLEM-SOLVING STRATEGY

Act It Out

Find the perimeter and area of the shape

To find the perimeter, you need
to measure each side of the shape.
Use a centimeter ruler or count.
Write the numbers below.

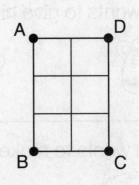

A to B __3__ cm   C to D __3__ cm

B to C __2__ cm   A to D __2__ cm

Then add the sides to find the perimeter.

__3__ + __2__ + __3__ + __2__ = __10__ The perimeter is __10__ cm.

Count the squares inside the shape to find the area.

The area is __6__ square units.

_____

Find the perimeter and area.

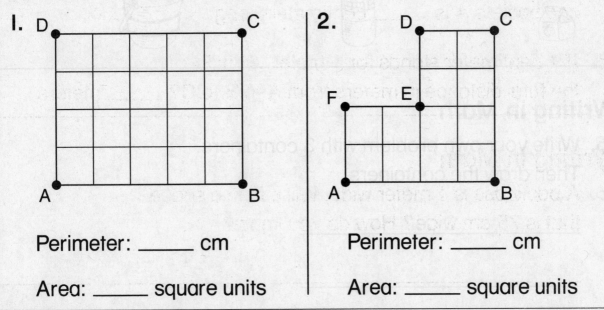

I.

Perimeter: _____ cm

Area: _____ square units

2.

Perimeter: _____ cm

Area: _____ square units

Using the page Help children *plan* each problem by asking them to find the lengths of each side. Then have
children add all the lengths to *solve*.

Understanding Capacity

Choose the best container.

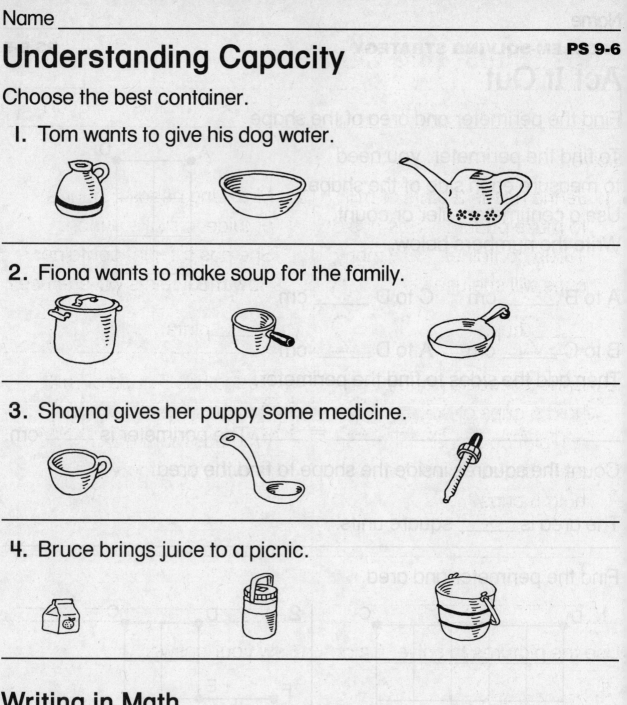

1. Tom wants to give his dog water.

2. Fiona wants to make soup for the family.

3. Shayna gives her puppy some medicine.

4. Bruce brings juice to a picnic.

Writing in Math

5. Write your own problem with 3 containers.
   Then draw the containers.

_____

_____

_____

Cups, Pints, and Quarts

2 cups = 1 pint	4 cups = 2 pints = 1 quart

Solve.

1. Jenna needs 2 pints of milk to make pudding. She has a 1-cup container. How many cups will she use?

_____ cups

2. Mrs. Ling needs 2 quarts of juice to make punch. She has a 1-pint container. How many pints will she use?

_____ pints

3. Enrico needs a pot that will hold 6 cups of soup. He has a 1-pint container. How can he figure out which pot will hold 6 cups?

_____

_____

4. Deena has 5 cups of milk. Troy has 2 pints of milk. Who has more milk? How do you know?

_____

_____

Use the pictures to solve. Color to show your answer.

5.

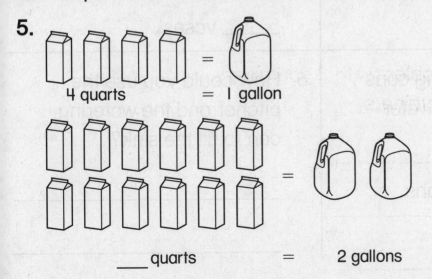

4 quarts = 1 gallon

____ quarts = 2 gallons

Name _____

Liters

The chart shows how many liters of water
some containers can hold.

Capacity in Liters

Container	 Pitcher	 Vase	 Watering Can	 Fish Tank	 Sink	 Tub
Number of Liters	1	5	10	15	23	40

Solve.

1. How many liters of water
   does it take to fill the
   watering can and the tub?

   _____ liters

2. How many liters of water
   does it take to fill the
   pitcher and the sink?

   _____ liters

3. How many more liters does
   it take to fill the tub than
   the vase?

   _____ liters

4. How many vases could you
   fill with water from
   the fish tank?

   _____ vases

5. How many watering cans
   could you fill with water
   from the tub?

   _____ watering cans

6. How could you use the
   pitcher and the watering
   can to fill the sink?

   _____

   _____

Understanding Volume

How many more cubes are needed to fill each box?

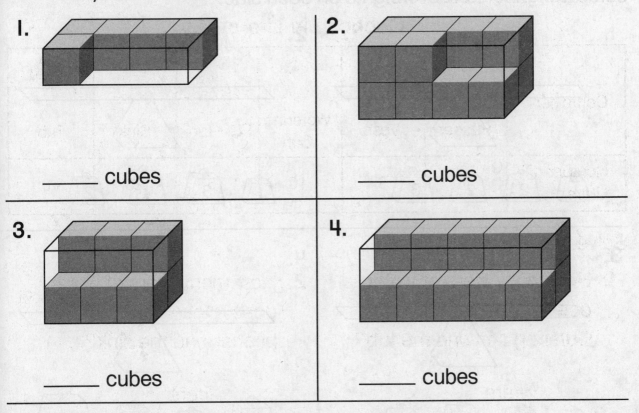

1. _____ cubes

2. _____ cubes

3. _____ cubes

4. _____ cubes

5. Look for the pattern. How many cubes would it take to make the next figure?

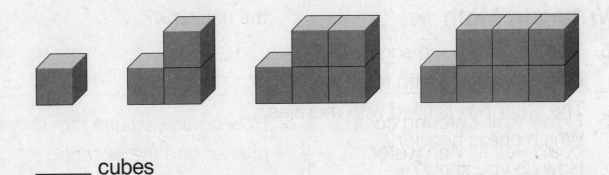

_____ cubes

Understanding Weight

Look at the pictures. Balance each scale
by drawing the correct weights on each side.

1.

2.

3.

4.

Writing in Math

5. Two boxes are the same size.

   One box is filled with feathers.

   The other box is filled with marbles.

   Which one is heavier?

   How do you know?

   _____

   _____

Pounds and Ounces

Circle the correct answers.
Remember, there are 16 ounces in 1 pound.

1. Anna puts 1 pound of bananas and some apples on the scale. Altogether they weigh more than 2 pounds. Which fruit weighs more?

bananas   apples

2. Freddy wants to make some sauce for his family. Does he use 5 pounds or 5 ounces of tomatoes?

5 pounds   5 ounces

3. Jake puts 18 ounces of carrots in a pot of soup and a pound of celery. Which weighs more, the carrots or the celery?

carrots   celery

4. Dixie makes a pumpkin pie. Does she use a 10-pound pumpkin or a 10-ounce pumpkin?

10-pound   10-ounce

5. Carla needs 2 pounds of flour to make some dough. She has a 30-ounce bag. Does she have enough flour? Tell how you know.

16 ounces = 1 pound

_____ ounces = 2 pounds

_____

_____

Grams and Kilograms

Circle the correct answers.

1. A cat measures about 6 kilograms. Which two animals together measure about the same as the cat?

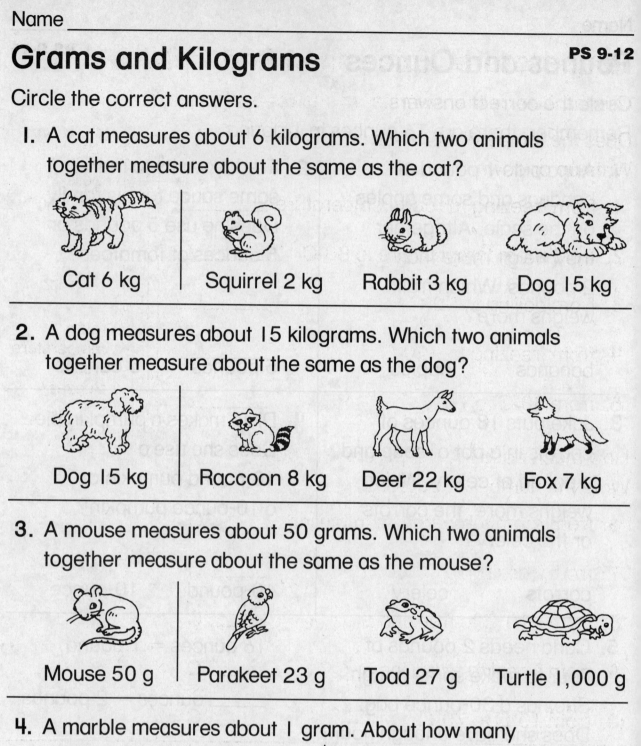

| Cat 6 kg | Squirrel 2 kg | Rabbit 3 kg | Dog 15 kg |

2. A dog measures about 15 kilograms. Which two animals together measure about the same as the dog?

| Dog 15 kg | Raccoon 8 kg | Deer 22 kg | Fox 7 kg |

3. A mouse measures about 50 grams. Which two animals together measure about the same as the mouse?

| Mouse 50 g | Parakeet 23 g | Toad 27 g | Turtle 1,000 g |

4. A marble measures about 1 gram. About how many marbles would it take to make $\frac{1}{2}$ of a kilogram?

1,000 g = 1 kg

_____ marbles

Temperature: Fahrenheit and Celsius

Use the Celsius thermometer to answer each question.

Does the temperature go up or down?
Write up or down.

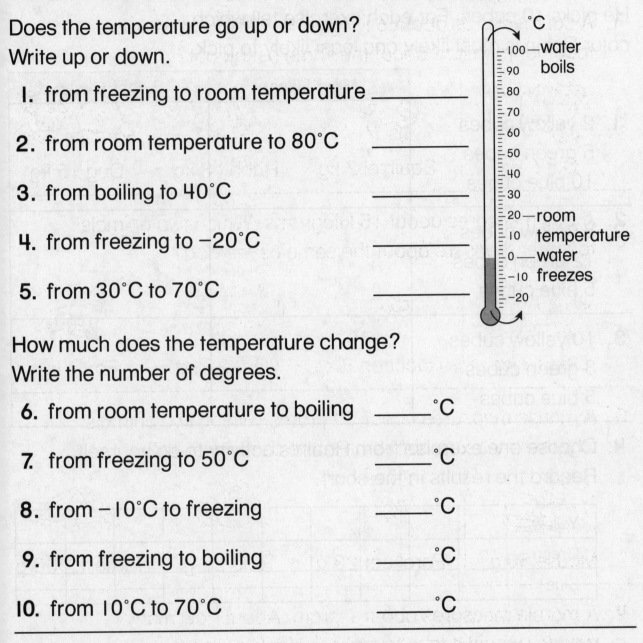

1. from freezing to room temperature _____

2. from room temperature to 80°C _____

3. from boiling to 40°C _____

4. from freezing to −20°C _____

5. from 30°C to 70°C _____

°C
— 100 — water
— 90   boils
— 80
— 70
— 60
— 50
— 40
— 30
— 20 — room
— 10   temperature
— 0 — water
— −10   freezes
— −20

How much does the temperature change?
Write the number of degrees.

6. from room temperature to boiling _____ °C

7. from freezing to 50°C _____ °C

8. from −10°C to freezing _____ °C

9. from freezing to boiling _____ °C

10. from 10°C to 70°C _____ °C

Writing in Math

11. Tell about the things you could do if it is 5°C outside.

_____

_____

Understanding Probability

Robin puts different colors of cubes in a bag.
He picks 10 cubes. For each exercise tell which
color Robin is most likely and least likely to pick.

	Most Likely	Least Likely
1. 2 yellow cubes 5 green cubes 10 blue cubes		
2. 8 yellow cubes 12 green cubes 5 blue cubes		
3. 10 yellow cubes 3 green cubes 5 blue cubes		

4. Choose one exercise from Robin's activity to do yourself.
Record the results in the chart.

Yellow										
Green										
Blue										

5. Which color did you pick the most? _____

_____

6. Which color did you pick the least? _____

_____

7. Do your results match your
answers for Robin's activity? _____

Using Probability

Complete the sentences.
Write **probable, certain,** or **impossible** for each.

1. Rickie has a bag with
8 red marbles and
3 green marbles.

It is _____
that he will pick
a red marble.

2. Marina has a bag with
11 yellow cubes
and 5 red cubes.

It is _____
that she will pick either
a yellow or a red cube.

3. Serena has a bag with
9 purple blocks and
6 pink blocks.

It is _____
that she will pick
a green block.

4. Motar has a spinner with
1 red part and 4 blue parts.

It is _____
that he will spin blue.

5. Color the spinner so
it will be probable that
you will spin red.

6. Color the spinner so
it will be impossible
that you will spin red.

Name _____

Multiple-Step Problems

Peter has 28 apples.

He uses 10 apples to make a pie.

Step 1: Subtract.

$$28 - 10 = 18$$

Then he gets 4 more apples.
How many apples does he have now?

Step 2: Add.

$$18 + 4 = 22 \text{ apples}$$

Solve.

1. Sasha has a string 35 inches long.
   She cuts off 16 inches to make a necklace.

   Step 1: _____

   Then she cuts off 8 inches to make a bracelet.
   How many inches of string are left?

   Step 2: _____ inches

Mental Math

2. A tub contains 25 liters of water. José pours in
   10 more liters. Ming adds another 10 liters.
   How many liters of water are in the tub now?   _____ liters

---

Using the page Have students *look back* and identify the two steps for each problem. Then have them *check* to see that they solved both steps.

PROBLEM-SOLVING APPLICATIONS

How Do You Measure Up?

Look at the pictures of the ribbons.
How much longer is the first ribbon?
Use a centimeter ruler to find out.

What is the problem asking?

_____

The first ribbon is __7__ cm longer.

_____

Solve.

1. Estimate the length of the ribbon. Use an inch ruler to measure.

   Estimate. _____ inches   Measure. _____ inches

Writing in Math

2. Describe an object you like. Tell about its length
   and weight. Use centimeters and kilograms.

   _____

   _____

Using the page Have children **read** each problem. Then ask them what the problem is asking to make sure that
they **understand** the question.

Building 1,000

Use the table to solve each problem.

There are 100 crayons in one box. Fill in the rest of the chart.

Boxes	1	2	3	4	5
Crayons	100	200			

1. How many crayons are in 3 boxes? _____ crayons

2. How many crayons are in all 5 boxes? _____ crayons

3. Jack takes 1 box of crayons.
   How many crayons are left? _____ crayons

There are 100 markers in one box. Fill in the rest of the chart.

Boxes	1	2	3	4	5	6	7	8
Markers	100	200	300	400	500			

4. How many markers are in 6 boxes? _____ markers

5. How many markers are in all 8 boxes? _____ markers

6. Viola adds one more box of markers.
   How many markers are there now? _____ markers

7. The school has 4 boxes of markers. They need
   1,000 markers in all. How many more markers
   does the school need?

   $400 +$ _____ $= 1,000$ The school needs _____ more markers.

Counting Hundreds, Tens, and Ones

Use the clues to write the number.

1. There is a 5 in the hundreds digit, a 6 in the tens digit, and a 3 in the ones digit.

What number is it? _____

2. There is a 2 in the ones digit, a 9 in the tens digit, and a 4 in the hundreds digit.

What number is it? _____

3. There are 7 tens, 4 ones, and 8 hundreds.

What number is it? _____

4. There are 6 ones, 5 hundreds, and 1 ten.

What number is it? _____

5. There are 3 hundreds, 9 ones, and 7 tens.

What number is it? _____

6. There are 6 ones and 2 hundreds.

What number is it? _____

7. Write all the three-digit numbers you can make using the digits 1, 7, and 5.

_____

_____

_____

8. Write all the three-digit numbers you can make using the digits 4, 2, and 8.

_____

_____

_____

Writing Numbers to 1,000

Use the chart to answer each question.

Number of Pages in Each School Book

Math	Science	Social Studies	Reading	Music
608	365	214	390	198

Write the name of the book with the following
number of pages.

1. $200 + 10 + 4$ _____

2. $100 + 90 + 8$ _____

3. $600 + 8$ _____

4. $300 + 60 + 5$ _____

5. Look at the number of pages in your math book.
   Write the number in expanded form.

   _____ + _____ + _____

6. Eight books each have 100 pages.
   How many pages is that in all?

   _____ pages

Changing Numbers by Hundreds and Tens

Solve each problem.

1. Roy drives 382 miles. Then he drives another 100 miles. How many miles does Roy drive altogether?

    _____ miles

2. 165 people are in line. 20 more people get in line. How many people are in line now?

    _____ people

3. 279 people go on a train trip. 30 people get off the train. How many people are still on the train?

    _____ people

4. 314 people are on an airplane. At the first stop, 100 people get off. How many people are still on the airplane?

    _____ people

5. Tasia drives 478 miles to the beach. Then she drives another 200 miles. How many miles does she drive altogether?

    _____ miles

6. A boat travels 641 miles to one port. Then it travels another 300 miles to another port. How many miles does the boat travel in all?

    _____ miles

7. 485 people are on a ship. At one stop, 50 people get off the ship. How many people are still on the ship?

    _____ people

Name _____

Comparing Numbers

Compare. Write >, <, or =.
Then answer the questions.

1. Doug has 125 pennies in his piggy bank.
   Amy has 458 pennies in her piggy bank.
   Whose piggy bank has more pennies?

   125 ◯ 458 _____

2. Mom's book has 215 pages.
   Dad's book has 680 pages.
   Whose book has fewer pages?

   215 ◯ 680 _____

3. Ellie's album has 409 pictures.
   Derek's album has 229 pictures.
   Derek adds 180 more pictures to his album.
   Whose album has more pictures?

   409 ◯ 409 _____

4. Use numbers to compare how many children
   the buses can hold. Write >, <, or =.

   ____ ◯ ____

Name _____

Parts of 1,000

Use the chart to solve each problem.

Sewing Supplies

Sewing Needles	Safety Pins	Spools of Thread	Straight Pins	Buttons
250	400	150	550	300

Mr. Wing needs 1,000 of each item in the chart.
Write a number sentence to find how many more
of each item Mr. Wing needs.

1. Sewing needles $\underline{\;250\;}$ + _____ = 1,000

   _____ more sewing needles

2. Buttons _____ + _____ = 1,000

   _____ more buttons

3. Spools of thread _____ + _____ = 1,000

   _____ more spools of thread

4. Straight pins _____ + _____ = 1,000

   _____ more straight pins

5. How many more safety pins are needed to make
   1,000? Skip count by 100s to find the answer.

   400, _____, _____, _____, _____, _____, 1,000

   _____ more safety pins are needed.

Name _____

Use Data from a Chart

You can use a chart to solve problems.

Grade 1 collected 100 more cans.
They forgot to add this to their total.
How many cans did they collect altogether?

What is the problem asking you to do?

Cans Collected on Recycling Day	
Grade 1	267
Grade 2	430
Grade 3	290
Grade 4	378

Add 100 to the total for Grade 1 to find
how many cans they collected in all.

What numbers will you use? _____ 100 and 267

What is the answer? _____ 367 cans

Use the chart to solve.

1. On the next day, Grade 2 collects two hundred more cans. Now how many cans do they have?

_____ cans

2. Grade 3 collects 50 + 4 more cans on the next day. How many cans did they collect for both days?

_____ cans

3. Grade 4 cannot recycle 100 cans. The remaining cans are recycled. How many cans did Grade 4 recycle? Write the answer in expanded form.

_____ cans

Using the page After children *read* the problem, have them explain the problem in their own words to help them *understand* what is being asked.

Before, After, and Between

Use the clues to find each number.
Write the numbers on the doors.

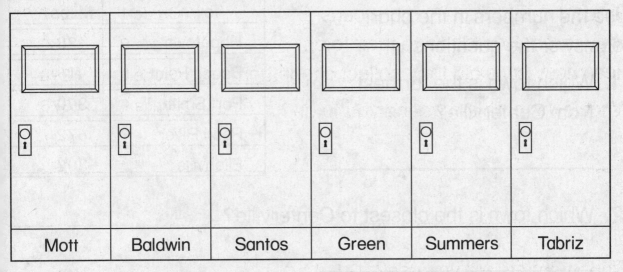

| Mott | Baldwin | Santos | Green | Summers | Tabriz |

1. The number on Miss Baldwin's door is before 370 and after 359. It has 8 ones. What number is it?

2. The number on Mr. Green's door is between 813 and 823. It has 7 ones. What number is it?

3. The number on Ms. Summers's door is after 500 and before 600. The number has 4 tens and 0 ones. What number is it?

4. The number on Mrs. Santos's door is between 200 and 230. It has the same number of hundreds, tens, and ones. What number is it?

5. The number on Miss Tabriz's door is between 600 and 650. The number has 4 ones and 1 ten. What number is it?

6. The number on Mr. Mott's door is after 100. If you count by 20s four times, you will get the number. What number is it?

Name _____

Ordering Numbers

This chart tells how many miles
each town is from Centerville.
Use the numbers in the chart
to answer the questions.

Distance from Centerville

Town	Miles
Hopetown	128
Beach Point	416
Port Smith	390
Pearl River	672
Ellenville	302

1. Which town is the farthest
   from Centerville?

   _____

2. Which town is the closest to Centerville?

   _____

3. Write the number of miles in order from least to greatest.

   _____ , _____ , _____ , _____ , _____

4. Write the little towns in order from the farthest from
   Centerville to the nearest to Centerville.

   _____ , _____ , _____ ,

   _____ , _____

Writing in Math

5. Write a question about
   ordering using the map.

   _____

   _____

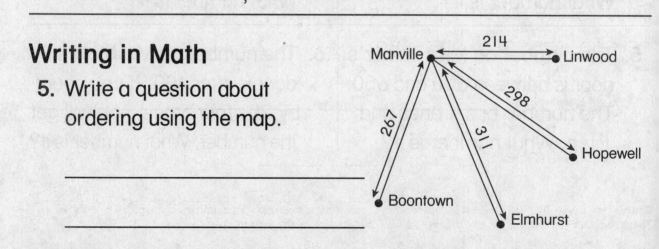

Name _____

Look for a Pattern

Read and Understand

Find the number that comes next.

215, 315, 415, 515, 615, ___?___

Plan and Solve

Look for a pattern rule. What is different about each number?

The hundreds digit changes each time.

How does the number change? It increases by 100.

So, the next number in the pattern will follow the same rule.

The next number in the pattern is __715__.

Look Back and Check

In your own words, what is the pattern rule?

Does your answer match the pattern rule?

_____

Describe the pattern rule. Write the numbers that come next.

1. 400, 375, 350, 325, 300, ___?___, ___?___, ___?___

Pattern rule _____

Next numbers _____, _____, _____

Using the page To help children *plan and solve,* have them decide how the numbers in the pattern change.
Then have them determine if the numbers increase or decrease by the amount they change.

Name _____

Rescue Vehicles

A lifeboat traveled 137 miles to a rescue.
Then it traveled another 100 miles to a larger boat.
How many miles did the lifeboat travel?

137 + 100 = ___237___

Check your answer. What did the problem ask you to do?

Find how many miles the lifeboat
traveled in all.

Does your answer solve the problem? ___yes___

Solve.

1. There were 156 firefighters at a fire.
   How many is 10 firefighters less?   _____ firefighters

   How many is 10 firefighters more?   _____ firefighters

2. Firehouse A responded to 187 alarms.
   Firehouse B responded to 215 alarms.
   Compare these two numbers.   _____ ◯ _____

Writing in Math

3. Write a number story about a   _____
   rescue. Use two 3-digit numbers.
   Compare the numbers.   _____

Using the page Ask children to *look back* and reread the problem. Then have them *check* that they solved the problem correctly.

Using Mental Math

Points Scored at Pinball

Nina	Kobe	Marsha	Anna	Sulu	Roberto
436	234	412	341	617	563

Use mental math to solve.

1. Nina and Marsha are on one team.
   How many points do they score?   _____ + _____ = _____

2. Kobe and Roberto are on one team.
   How many points do they score?   _____ + _____ = _____

3. Anna and Sulu are on one team.
   How many points do they score?   _____ + _____ = _____

4. Two players from different teams
   score a total of 575 points. One of the
   players is Kobe. Who is the other player?   _____

5. Which team scored the most points?

   _____

6. Which team scored the least points?

   _____

Name _____

Estimating Sums

Estimate to solve.

1. Mindy's Vegetable Stand has 213 red tomatoes
   and 323 green tomatoes. Does she have
   more than or less than 500 tomatoes?

   _____ 500 tomatoes

2. Sue's Sewing Store has 185 large buttons and
   201 small buttons. Does Sue's shop have
   more than or less than 300 buttons?

   _____ 300 buttons

3. Rob's Art Shop has 328 water color paints
   and 215 oil paints. Does Rob's shop have
   more than or less than 600 paints?

   _____ 600 paints

Circle the correct answer.

4. Ms. Walsh's Health Food Bar has 425 boxes
   of hot cereal and some boxes of cold cereal.
   In all, there are about 500 boxes of cereal.
   How many boxes of cold cereal are there?

   150   200   100

Name _____

Adding with Models

Solve. Use models to find each sum.

1. Leo drives 415 miles to Oakland, then another 231 miles to Fairview. How many miles does he drive?

   _____ + _____ = _____ miles

2. Olivia flies 516 miles to Greenville, then drives another 148 miles. How many miles does she travel in all?

   _____ + _____ = _____ miles

3. A train travels 221 miles by day and 347 miles at night. How many miles does the train travel in all?

   _____ + _____ = _____ miles

4. A bus tour travels 472 miles on Thursday and 283 miles on Friday. How far does the bus travel in two days?

   _____ + _____ = _____ miles

Circle the best estimate.

5. Mrs. Pinky sails 256 miles on her boat to an island. Then she sails 139 miles to another island. About how many miles does she sail in all?

   300   400   500

6. Mr. DeLuca hikes 192 miles in one week. Then he hikes 173 miles the next week. About how many miles does Mr. DeLuca hike in two weeks?

   200   300   400

Adding Three-Digit Numbers

Add.

1. $\begin{array}{r} 362 \\ +143 \\ \hline \end{array}$ $\begin{array}{r} 418 \\ +290 \\ \hline \end{array}$ $\begin{array}{r} 167 \\ +482 \\ \hline \end{array}$ $\begin{array}{r} 237 \\ +156 \\ \hline \end{array}$ $\begin{array}{r} 643 \\ +215 \\ \hline \end{array}$

2. $\begin{array}{r} 167 \\ +131 \\ \hline \end{array}$ $\begin{array}{r} 451 \\ +\ 62 \\ \hline \end{array}$ $\begin{array}{r} 347 \\ +112 \\ \hline \end{array}$ $\begin{array}{r} 266 \\ +324 \\ \hline \end{array}$ $\begin{array}{r} 128 \\ +205 \\ \hline \end{array}$

Circle the numbers on the tic-tac-toe boards
that match the sums from Exercises 1 and 2.
The player that gets 3 in a row or in a diagonal, wins.

Player A

708	649	127
316	291	858
513	483	590

Player B

333	678	411
176	505	393
298	843	459

3. Which player wins tic-tac-toe? _____

4. Look at the board of the winning player.
   Which two circled numbers will make
   the greatest sum when added together?

   _____ + _____ = _____

Practice with Three-Digit Addition

The table shows how many miles there are between
cities. Use the table to solve each problem below.

	Port Smith	Lakeside	Greenville	New Hope
Port Smith		414	(291)	365
Lakeside	414		529	152
Greenville	291	529		(327)
New Hope	365	152	327	

---

1. Jenny goes from Port Smith to Greenville,
then from Greenville to New Hope.
How far does she travel?

_____ miles

$$\begin{array}{r} 291 \\ +327 \\ \hline \end{array}$$

---

2. Miguel goes from New Hope to Lakeside,
then from Lakeside to Port Smith.
How far does he travel?

_____ miles

---

3. Ben goes from Greenville to New Hope,
then from New Hope to Port Smith.
How far does he go?

_____ miles

---

4. Shi-Ann goes from Lakeside to Greenville.
Then she travels to another city.
She travels a total of 856 miles.
Where does she go to from Greenville? _____

Name _____

Make a Graph

How many tickets were sold on each day? Add the numbers for each day and write the totals in the chart.

Tickets Sold for the Movies			
	Friday	Saturday	Sunday
Booth A	150	300	200
Booth B	200	350	300
Total			

Use the totals to make a graph.

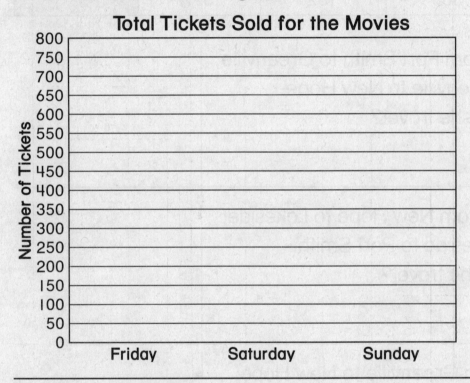

Total Tickets Sold for the Movies

Writing in Math

1. How can you use your graph to find out how many people went to the movies each day?

_____

_____

Using the page To help children *plan,* have them circle the numbers for each day, then add. Then have them *solve* by coloring in the bars on the graph.

Ways to Find Missing Parts

Ms. Murple needs to buy more items for her craft store. She wants to have a certain number of each item in the store. Count on or count back to find how many of each item she needs to buy.

Complete the chart.

1.

Ms. Murple's Craft Supplies

	Pipe Cleaners	Craft Paper	Colored Pencils	Boxes of Beads	Silk Flowers
Number in the Store	140	270	350	180	430
Number Needed	_____	_____	_____	_____	_____
Number Wanted	500	800	600	300	900

Use the pictures to solve.

2. Ms. Murple needs to fill a carton with 500 paint jars. She only has four small boxes that hold 50 paint jars each. How many more small boxes of paint jars does she need to fill the carton?

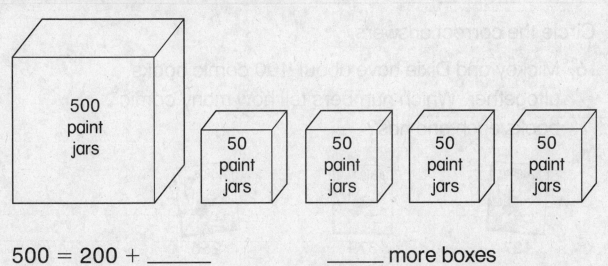

500 = 200 + _____   _____ more boxes

Name _____

Estimating Differences

Match the number sentence with the estimate.

1. Sue and Roger collect coins. Sue has about 300 more coins than Roger.

591 − 482

2. Beth and David collect baseball cards. David has about 400 more cards than Beth.

623 − 198

3. Raif and Andrea collect marbles. Andrea has about 100 more marbles than Raif.

743 − 416

4. Suey and Ahmad collect seashells. Ahmad has about 200 more shells than Suey.

932 − 387

5. Greta and Zack collect postcards. Greta has about 500 more postcards than Zack.

417 − 226

Circle the correct answers.

6. Mickey and Dixie have about 400 comic books altogether. Which numbers tell how many comic books each one has?

127

374

266

Subtracting with Models

Solve. Use models and Workmat 5 to find
each difference.

1. A truck carries 578 boxes. It takes
   243 boxes to a store. How many
   boxes are still on the truck?   _____ − _____ = _____

2. A train carries 635 pounds of hay.
   It unloads 214 pounds. How many
   pounds of hay are still on the train?   _____ − _____ = _____

3. A barge carries 792 cartons. It unloads
   350 cartons at the dock. How many
   cartons are still on the barge?   _____ − _____ = _____

4. A plane carries 469 pounds
   of cargo. It unloads 325 pounds
   at the first stop. How many pounds
   of cargo are still on the plane?   _____ − _____ = _____

Find the answer.

5. A plane, a train, and a truck each carry cartons.
   The plane carries about 500 more cartons than
   the train. The train carries the least number of
   cartons. How many cartons does each one carry?

295
450
780

_____   _____   _____

Subtracting Three-Digit Numbers

Subtract. Write the letter for each difference
on the lines below to solve the riddle.

1. 462 −136	925 −184	776 −236	387 −149	591 −204
R	E	C	D	F
2. 657 −482	824 −193	475 −293	656 −243	927 −371
N	A	L	O	I

3. What has ears but cannot hear?

___ ___ ___ ___ ___ ___ ___ ___ ___ ___
631   540   413   326   175   387   556   741   182   238

Solve.

4. The bags below are filled with jellybeans.
   Allie uses 245 jellybeans.
   How many jellybeans are left?

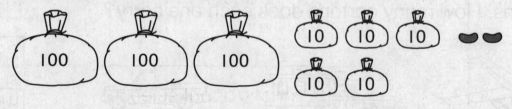

_____ jellybeans

Name _____

Practice with Three-Digit Subtraction

The table shows how many books
of each kind are at the town library.
Use the table to solve the problems.

Number of Books	
Fiction	672
Places	328
People	576
Science	441
Art	255

1. How many more books about people
   are there than books about places?

   _____ more books

---

2. How many more fiction books
   are there than art books?

   _____ more books

---

3. 170 of the science books are about
   animals. How many science books
   are not about animals?

   _____ books

---

4. 192 of the fiction books are about people
   from other countries. How many fiction
   books are about people from our country?

   _____ books

---

5. The library gets another 135 books about science.
   Are there more than or less than
   500 books about science now?   _____ 500 books

Name _____

Exact Answer or Estimate

Riuchi has 573 newspapers. She delivers 128 newspapers on her paper route. How many newspapers does Riuchi have left?

Do you need an exact answer? Can you estimate?

You need to find how many newspapers are left. You need an exact answer.

> Think: Riuchi takes away 128 newspapers from 573 newspapers. This is a subtraction problem.

$$\begin{array}{r} 5\ 7\ 3 \text{ newspapers} \\ -\ 1\ 2\ 8 \text{ are taken away.} \\ \hline 4\ 4\ 5 \text{ newspapers are left.} \end{array}$$

Circle **estimate** or **exact answer.**
Answer the questions. Show your work.

1. 423 people work at the newspaper company. About 200 people take the bus to work. About how many people do not take the bus to work?

   estimate

   exact answer

   _____

2. A reporter travels 249 miles to cover a story. Then the reporter travels another 135 miles. How many miles does the reporter travel in all?

   estimate

   exact answer

   _____

Using the page Have children *look back* to see if they circled estimate or exact answer. Then have them *check* the problem to make sure they are correct.

Name _____

Amazing Animals

A jaguar runs for 417 feet. A puma runs for 253 feet.
How many more feet does the jaguar run?

What is the question asking?

How many more feet the
jaguar runs than the puma.

Do you add or subtract? ___subtract___

$$\begin{array}{r} \overset{3}{\cancel{4}}\overset{11}{\cancel{1}}7 \\ -253 \\ \hline 164 \end{array}$$

The jaguar runs __164__ more feet than a puma.

Solve.

1. There are 563 ants in a colony.
   246 ants leave to look for food.
   How many ants are still in the colony? _____ ants

Writing in Math

2. A baby gorilla weighs 87 pounds. Another baby gorilla weighs
   62 pounds. The mother gorilla weighs 295 pounds. Do the baby
   gorillas together weigh more than the mother? How do you know?

   _____

   _____

Using the page Have children *read* each problem. Then have them tell what the problem is asking to show that
they *understand* the problem.

Skip Counting Equal Groups

Draw a picture to solve. Write how many in all.

1. Hannah has 3 groups of 2 balloons. How many balloons does she have in all?

   _____ balloons in all

2. Jed has 4 groups of 4 party hats. How many party hats does he have in all?

   _____ party hats in all

3. Latrell has 2 groups of 5 stickers. How many stickers does he have in all?

   _____ stickers in all

4. Aliza has 5 groups of 3 cups. How many cups does she have in all?

   _____ cups in all

Writing in Math

5. Write a word problem about 3 groups of 4. Solve the problem. Draw a picture to show the groups.

   _____

   _____

Repeated Addition and Multiplication

Write an addition sentence and a multiplication sentence
for each part of the problem. Draw pictures if you need help.

1. Ms. Marple is making punch. She needs to mix 3 cups of cider,
   2 cups of orange juice, and 5 cups of soda water to make one bowl.

   If she makes 3 bowls of punch, how
   many cups of cider does she need?

   ____ + ____ + ____ = ____   ____ × ____ = ____

   How many cups of orange juice does
   she need to make 3 bowls of punch?

   ____ + ____ + ____ = ____   ____ × ____ = ____

   How many cups of soda water does
   she need to make 3 bowls of punch?

   ____ + ____ + ____ = ____   ____ × ____ = ____

2. Mr. Marple mixes 3 cups of flour with granola
   and milk to make one loaf of bread. How many
   cups of flour does he need to make 4 loaves?

   ____ + ____ + ____ + ____ = ____

   ____ × ____ = ____

3. Mr. Marple uses 2 cups of milk to make one loaf of bread.
   Circle the number sentence that shows how many cups
   of milk he would need to make 5 loaves of bread.

   $5 \times 1 = 5$ $5 \times 2 = 10$ $5 \times 3 = 15$

Name _____

Building Arrays

This is what the windows in Billy's Sports Shop look like.

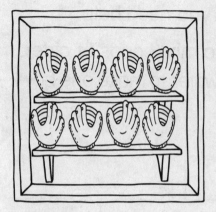  

Write a multiplication sentence to answer each question.

I. How many baseball mitts are there in all?	**2.** How many balls are there in all?
_____ × _____ = _____	_____ × _____ = _____
3. Billy adds 2 more baseball caps to each row. Draw what the display looks like now. Write a multiplication sentence.	**4.** Billy adds another row of baseball mitts. Draw what the display looks like now. Write a multiplication sentence.
_____ × _____ = _____	_____ × _____ = _____

Multiplying in Any Order

Draw 2 pictures showing different ways to group.
Write the multiplication sentences.

1. Gabby has 6 pictures.
   Show two ways
   she can arrange
   the pictures in
   an array.

   ___ × ___ = ___ | ___ × ___ = ___

2. Jacob has 10 stamps
   to put in a stamp album.
   Show two ways
   he can arrange the
   stamps in an array.

   ___ × ___ = ___ | ___ × ___ = ___

Use the array to complete the number sentences.
Write the missing numbers.

3.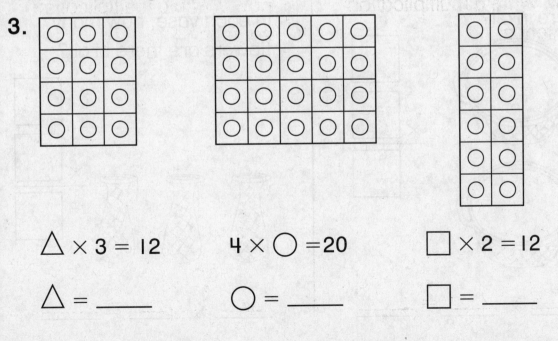

   $\triangle \times 3 = 12$ $4 \times \bigcirc = 20$ $\square \times 2 = 12$

   $\triangle = $ _____ $\bigcirc = $ _____ $\square = $ _____

Name _____

Vertical Form

Draw a picture to solve. Multiply across and down.

1. There are 3 pencil holders with 3 pencils in each holder. How many pencils are there in all?

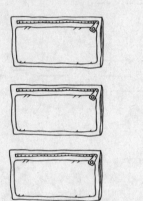

_____ × _____ = _____

2. There are 2 tanks with 5 fish in each tank. How many fish are there in all?

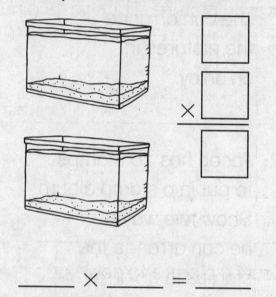

_____ × _____ = _____

3. There are 2 baskets with 6 apples in each basket. How many apples are there in all?

_____ × _____ = _____

4. There are 3 vases with 4 flowers in each vase. If Tricia puts one more flower in each vase, how many flowers are there in all?

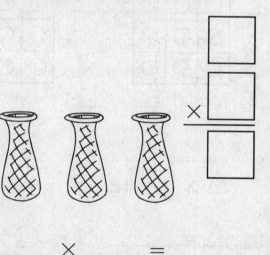

_____ × _____ = _____

Name _____

Draw a Picture

Dexter has 5 boxes.

He packs 3 balls in each box.

How many balls does he pack in all?

Draw a picture. Then write a number sentence to solve.

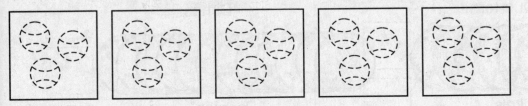

Did you draw a picture of 3 balls in each box?

_____

Draw a picture to solve each problem.

Then write a multiplication sentence.

1. Lucy has 4 boxes. She packs
    5 yo-yos in each box. How many
    yo-yos does she pack in all?

    _____ × _____ = _____

_____

2. Yancy has 3 boxes. He packs
    3 tops in each box. How many
    tops does he pack in all?

    _____ × _____ = _____

_____

Using the page To help children **look back,** have them reread each problem, then **check** their pictures to see if
they match the numbers in the problem.

Making Equal Groups

Count the coins.

Use the number of coins to solve each problem.

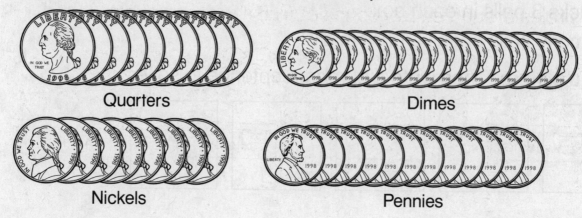

Quarters

Dimes

Nickels

Pennies

1. How many quarters in all? _____
   How can 2 children equally share the quarters?

   Each child gets _____ quarters.

2. How many nickels in all? _____
   How can 4 children equally share the nickels?

   Each child gets _____ nickels.

3. Write 2 ways you can equally share the pennies.

   _____ groups of _____

   _____ groups of _____

4. Write 2 ways you can equally share the dimes.

   _____ groups of _____

   _____ groups of _____

Writing Division Sentences

Count how many there are of each fruit.

Write division sentences to show equal shares.

Draw circles around equal groups of fruit if you need help.

1. Karen puts the pears into 6 boxes.

   How many pears go in each box?

   _____ ÷ _____ = _____

2. Wendall puts the strawberries in 4 cartons.

   How many strawberries go in each carton?

   _____ ÷ _____ = _____

3. Anna puts the apples in 3 baskets.

   How many apples go in each basket?

   _____ ÷ _____ = _____

4. Willy gets 3 more lemons. Can he put an
   equal number of lemons in 2 boxes? Explain.

   _____

   _____

Name _____

Choose an Operation

Melly collects stickers. She puts 6 stickers
on each page in her book. She fills 4 pages
with stickers. How many stickers are there in all?

What operation will you use to solve this problem?

Will you add, subtract, or multiply? __multiply__

$6 + 4 = 12$ $6 - 4 = 2$ $(6 \times 4 = 24)$

Why do you think you will __multiply__?

__Because each page is a group of stickers.__

There are __24__ stickers in all.

_____

Circle the number sentence that solves the problem.

1. Kareem collects 5 model cars.
   He gives 2 cars to his friend.
   How many cars does Kareem
   have now?   Kareem has _____ cars.

   $5 - 2 = 3$ $5 + 2 = 7$ $5 \times 2 = 10$

_____

2. Nadia collects 20 finger puppets.
   She puts an equal number of
   puppets on 4 shelves. How many   There are _____ puppets
   puppets are on each shelf?   on each shelf.

   $20 \div 4 = 5$ $20 - 4 = 16$ $20 + 4 = 24$

_____

Using the page To help children *plan* and *solve* each problem, ask them to estimate if their answer will be a
small or large number.

PROBLEM-SOLVING APPLICATIONS

Up, Up, and Away!

A plane has 127 passengers.

At one stop, 82 more passengers get on the plane.

How many passengers are on the plane now?

What numbers will you use?

127 and 82
_____

$127 + 82 =$ _209_   _209_ passengers in all

Solve.

1. There are 65 suitcases on a baggage cart. 25 suitcases are loaded onto a plane. How many suitcases are still on the cart?

    _____ − _____ = _____

2. A plane makes 3 trips in one day. How many trips does the plane make in one week?

    _____ × _____ = _____

Writing in Math

3. Write a division story about airplanes.

_____

_____

_____

Using the page To help children *read and understand*, ask them to tell the numbers they will use to write each number sentence.

Use with Lesson 12-10.   **159**